Human Relations for
Office Workers:
A Case Approach

Human Relations for Office Workers:
A Case Approach

Calfrey C. Calhoun
Alton V. Finch
The University of Georgia

44777

CHARLES E. MERRILL PUBLISHING COMPANY
A Bell & Howell Company
Columbus, Ohio

International Standard Book Number: 0-675-09118-7

Library of Congress Catalog Card Number: 71-186553

1 2 3 4 5 6 7 8 - 77 76 75 74 73 72
Printed in the United States of America

PREFACE

This book represents a completely new concept in textbooks for training office workers, in that it provides an instructional sequence of sixteen case-incidents and thirty-nine critical incidents directly related to realistic office problems and actual job situations encountered by office workers today. The text is based on data from the recent U.S. Office of Education NOBELS (New Office and Business Education Learning System) Study, in which the authors participated, and it incorporates a series of exercises for developing human relations skills in office workers. The final NOBELS project consisted of an analysis of 829 social-interaction critical incidents, covering both effective and ineffective behaviors of office workers, which were collected nationwide from office supervisors. This correlative report represents the first systematic development of learning activities based on the critical social requirements of office work. It is part of an overall study to develop a new office and business education curriculum through on-site analysis of the job tasks and social-role requirements of 1232 office workers and their supervisors from four areas of the United States.

Developed in an easy-to-use semi-programmed format, the book is designed for several users. (1) Area vocational or technical school, community college, and college and university students and teachers in business education and related areas will find it a valuable supplementary text for such courses as Office Management, Business Communication, and directed work experience courses for students and teachers, as well as Business Curriculum and Methods of Teaching business education courses. (2) Vocational business education supervisors and directors, business teacher educators, and curriculum directors will find the materials a source of new ideas for the training of office workers and teachers. (3) Experienced on-the-job office employees, office managers, office trainees, supervisors, and directors of company office training programs will find the cases to be a means of putting across the essentials of human relations training in a concentrated period of time. (4) High school students and teachers will find it valuable in relating classroom instruction (in such courses as Office Practice, Vocational Office Training, Supervised Work Experience, General Business, and Business Organization and Management) to actual office skills and procedures.

Office workers who have worked full-time or part-time will recognize familiar office problems and will be eager to solve them. Students in training or about to enter the job market will develop improved traits and decision-making skills which will rapidly qualify them for work. Students in their first jobs will have the practical training that office managers want.

The materials developed in the text were pilot tested under the supervision of business education teachers in the Duval County Public Schools, Jacksonville, Fla., and subsequently revised.

Since it utilizes "live" material and draws upon newer methods of instruction, such as simulation and role playing, this book should result in improved instruction and renewed student interest and participation in the human relations component of office training.

March, 1972   *Calfrey C. Calhoun*

Alton V. Finch

CONTENTS

Human Relations for Office Workers:
A Case Approach

Part I

Relationships with Co-workers

ALMOST EVERYONE WORKS WITH SOMEONE ELSE. TO A LARGE EXTENT, how well members of a group work together will determine the success of an enterprise. Recent records indicate that when workers feel accepted by their work group they are less likely to be absent: working with the group is more satisfying to them than staying away from work.[1]

The ability to get along with other people is essential if an employee is to perform his job effectively. Not only must he adjust to the demands of his own position and to those of his supervisor; he must also develop good working relationships with his co-workers. Being considerate of other people's responsibilities and problems is as important as following proper office procedures; both contribute to the establishment of a spirit of cooperation which makes working both more pleasant and more efficient.

An office employee can grow, in a professional and personal sense, through self-analysis. In particular, he can improve his awareness of himself and of how he gets along with other people. Experience in dealing with other people and the ability to look at a situation objectively are both important factors in increasing this awareness. The case-incidents in this book present a variety of situations which an office employee might encounter; the material following each incident provides a guide for objective analysis. Therefore, by studying each incident carefully, the reader will be able to increase his own self-awareness.

Part I will focus on the following important characteristics desirable in office workers: *working under pressure, accepting responsibility, taking initiative,* and *using tact and good judgment.*

---

[1] Reproduced from *Psychology: Human Relations and Motivation,* 4th edition, by Donald A. Laird and Eleanor Laird, Copyright 1967, with permission of Gregg Division, McGraw-Hill Book Company, publishers and copyright owners.

TELEPHONE
TECHNIQUE

In this incident you will meet Cynthia Young who is temporarily confronted with the responsibility of simultaneously handling two tasks. Read the following selection to find out how well Cynthia works under pressure.

FOR THE PAST SIX MONTHS CYNTHIA YOUNG HAS BEEN EMPLOYED AS AN accounting clerk in the Business Office of Clark Central Hospital. Her major responsibilities include checking out patients and figuring charges, sending statements to former patients, and handling insurance claims. Occasionally, Cynthia has answered the telephone for co-workers and has sometimes failed to relay accurate information about who called or the information requested.

On Thursday afternoon, Cynthia offered to answer the telephone so that a co-worker, Martha Reynolds, could take a coffee break. Almost immediately, several patients came to the window to check out. The first man had several questions about his insurance policy. Cynthia noticed that the other patients were becoming impatient while she helped him.

Just then the telephone rang. Cynthia let it ring several times before she left the patient and answered it.

CYNTHIA: Hello

CALLER: Is this the Business Office?

CYNTHIA: Yes, this is Mr. Morgan's office.

CALLER: May I speak to him, please?

CYNTHIA: He's not in right now.

CALLER: When do you expect him back?

CYNTHIA: Oh, I don't know.

CALLER: Would you please have him call me back?

CYNTHIA: (looking for but not finding the telephone message pad) Okay.

CALLER: My number is 922-9786. This is Bill Harding. (pause) Did you get that?

CYNTHIA: (writing on a scrap of paper) Yes, I did. Goodbye. (Cynthia's scribbled message read: "Mr. Hardin/922-9678.")

Cynthia remembered the telephone call later in the afternoon and told Martha that someone had called Mr. Morgan and that she had left his name and phone number on Martha's desk. Mr. Morgan asked Martha to place the call. However, when she dialed the number she found that it was not in service. She was unable to get the number from the directory or from the information operator because she did not have either the first name or the initials of the caller and Cynthia did not remember them.

WHAT HAPPENS NEXT?

Write the resulting dialogue between (1) Mr. Morgan and Martha, and (2) Martha and Cynthia.

Analysis of Case-Incident

Fact: *Answer the following questions.*

1. What specific actions did Cynthia and Martha take when working under pressure? Did they respond well or poorly in each case?

2. What other characteristics of office workers are illustrated in this case?

3. List all the errors you can find in the telephone dialogue to support the proposition that Cynthia is weak in correct telephone technique.

Implications: *Indicate which of the following assumptions are valid.*
1. Good telephone usage was important in the office where Cynthia worked.
2. Cynthia did not like to be bothered with phone calls when she was busy.
3. Cynthia had had no formal training in telephone usage.
4. Cynthia was popular with her co-workers.
5. Cynthia frequently answered the telephone for Martha while she was on her coffee break.
6. Martha was Mr. Morgan's secretary.

Verification: *Indicate whether each of the following statements is true, false, or not discussed in the case-incident.*
1. Cynthia performs her regular tasks well.
2. Cynthia's co-workers have been displeased with her telephone techniques for some time.
3. Since Cynthia knew Mr. Harding she did not need to record his full name.

Thought: *Be prepared to answer each of the following questions.*
1. How might this situation have been avoided?
2. Where was Cynthia's first responsibility: to the customer at the window or to the person calling on the telephone? Why?
3. Was Martha at fault for leaving Cynthia to answer the telephone?
4. Why is good telephone technique important in the business office?
5. Why is complete accuracy necessary when taking telephone messages?
6. What should Cynthia have done to insure recording the correct message?
7. What should be included when one takes a telephone message?
8. Should Cynthia have been the one to end the conversation?
9. Do you think Cynthia's office used printed telephone pads?

Generalization: *Write a statement describing the type of person who could perform successfully in a situation such as the one Cynthia encountered.*

Activities

1. Obtain sample printed telephone message forms from several companies. What kinds of information does each include? (An alternate activity would be to design a telephone message form.)

2. Compare Cynthia's note to the forms obtained for Activity One. What essential information is missing from her message?

3. Using the evaluation form at the end of this section, rate Cynthia's telephone conversation.

4. Invite a representative from your telephone company to discuss proper telephone techniques.

5. Write dialogues for effective and ineffective phone calls. Other class members should (1) rate the calls using the evaluation form at the end of this section, and (2) attempt to fill out a message form based on each conversation. Use a Teletrainer (available from your local telephone company) to present the conversations to the class.

6. Write a skit about the telephone conversation in this case-incident. Reenact the telephone conversation with the use of a Teletrainer.

7. Write and tape a telephone conversation. Draw transparencies which show the individuals involved; display them while the tape is being played.

8. Design cartoon strips showing the possible reactions of the individuals involved in this case-incident.

9. Rewrite or reenact the conversation in this case-incident with improvements.

10. Create one cartoon character to be the character of the week for a cartoon strip to be placed on the bulletin board. It might provide a launching point from which such items as company loyalty, gossiping in the office, office clowns, etc., may be discussed. The main characters might be Chatty Cathy, Hazardous Harry, Moonlight Myron, and Rumors Rodney.

EVALUATION FORM
Person Answering a Business Call

	Satisfactory (check)	Unsatisfactory (check)
A. Beginning of the call.		
1. Answered promptly and pleasantly.	_____	_____
2. Gave proper identification.	_____	_____
B. Development of the call.		
1. Was attentive; displayed interest.	_____	_____
2. Used good judgment in deciding how to handle the situation.	_____	_____
3. Was alert to opportunities to be of assistance (transfer, call back, message).	_____	_____
4. Volunteered helpful information.	_____	_____
5. Gave explanations effectively.	_____	_____
6. Made inquiries tactfully.	_____	_____
7. Was prepared to take message.	_____	_____
8. Recorded necessary information carefully.	_____	_____
9. Verified information (spelling, figures, etc.).	_____	_____
10. Used proper techniques when necessary to leave the line.	_____	_____
C. Closing of the call.		
1. Left a pleasing impression at the close of the call.	_____	_____
2. Was certain that the conversation had been completed before replacing the receiver.	_____	_____
D. Voice personality.		
1. Spoke distinctly, directly into the mouthpiece.	_____	_____
2. Used correct grammar; avoided slang.	_____	_____
3. Injected polite expressions (please, thank you).	_____	_____
4. Reflected a friendly, sincere manner.	_____	_____
5. Acted with poise and confidence.	_____	_____
6. Gave the caller a feeling of assurance.	_____	_____
7. Represented the business courteously and efficiently.	_____	_____

Source: Teletraining for Business Studies. American Telephone and Telegraph Company, 1965. Courtesy of Southern Bell Telephone and Telegraph Company.

THE RELUCTANT SUPERVISOR

The change from running a one-man office to supervising additional office employees is difficult for some people. Read the following incident to find out how Glenn Weathers reacted.

SINCE GRADUATING FROM HIGH SCHOOL TWO YEARS AGO, GLENN Weathers has been employed by B & B Tax Service. He doubles as an accounting clerk and administrative assistant to the two accountants, Joe Boyce and Tom Boyer, who own the service. Each morning Glenn receives a list of the work to be done that day. It is his responsibility to see that it is completed.

Much of the time Glenn is left alone in the office, since it is necessary for the accountants to do the major portion of their work in the offices of their clients. During the months of January through April, however, additional clerical workers are hired to help out with the extra work. This year two girls were hired as temporary helpers. Since he is accustomed to a one-man office operation, Glenn is hesitant about giving the two girls directions. Occasionally he has stayed overtime to complete work the girls left unfinished.

Today is particularly hectic for Glenn because it is April 13 and there are only two days left before all the tax returns must be typed and ready for mailing. The two typists, Martha and Eunice, arrived at work fifteen minutes late. They had been at work only thirty minutes when Martha's boyfriend came by to take her out for a coffee break. Eunice took this opportunity to call her girl friend and tell her about the date she had had the night before. Then she also left for her break.

When the girls returned, it was almost eleven o'clock. Glenn realized that something would have to be done if the work were to be completed by five o'clock.

WHAT HAPPENS NEXT?

Describe in writing what action, if any, you think Glenn should take. Be prepared to justify your response.

Analysis of Case-Incident

Fact: *Answer the following questions.*
1. What specific actions of the office workers in this case-incident demonstrate accepting responsibility? What actions demonstrate avoiding responsibility?

2. What other characteristics of office workers are illustrated in this case?

3. What are Glenn's job duties?

4. List Glenn's weaknesses as an office worker and cite evidence to support each one.

Implications: *Indicate which of the following assumptions are valid.*
1. Glenn lacks the authority necessary to direct the work of temporary B & B employees.

2. Glenn appears to be an introvert.

3. Glenn is an efficient office employee.

4. Glenn appears to be an individual who likes to give orders.

5. Glenn is an efficient office manager.

6. Glenn does not like to supervise the work of others.

7. Glenn's difficulties with Martha and Eunice are symptoms of a more fundamental problem.

Verification: *Indicate whether each of the following statements is true, false, or not discussed in the case-incident.*
1. B & B Tax Service has no established company policy regarding coffee breaks.

2. At the time of employment, Martha and Eunice were briefed on office organization and procedure by Mr. Boyce and Mr. Boyer.

3. Glenn has had problems with Martha and Eunice since January.

Thought: *Be prepared to answer each of the following questions.*

1. Should temporary employees observe the same rules as permanent employees?

2. What is the reason for the difficulty in this case?

3. Does Glenn have the authority to direct the work of Martha and Eunice?

4. How can Glenn avoid such difficulty with temporary employees next year?

5. How will Mr. Boyce and Mr. Boyer react to Glenn's report of the incident?

6. How may your personal characteristics influence an employer to either hire you or refuse to hire you?

Generalization: *Write a statement describing the type of person who could perform successfully in a situation such as the one Glenn encountered.*

Activities

1. Write skits to dramatize the incident (a) as it actually happened, and (b) as it might have happened if Mr. Weathers had been an effective office manager.

2. Invite the personnel manager from a local temporary employment service to talk with the class about the training program and job opportunities for temporary office workers. (An alternative activity would be to tape the interview.)

3. Interview a local accountant or tax service representative to find out the qualifications and openings for temporary office help. Present your findings to the class.

4. Explore, through the library or through an interview with a vocational guidance counselor or a local businessman, the opportunities in the accounting field. Tape your interview and make a report to the class.

5. Define and give an example of the following four attributes:
   a. Punctuality
   b. Motivation
   c. Initiative
   d. Dependability

6. Which single attribute listed in Activity Five do you feel is most important when an employer is considering hiring a worker? Justify your answer.

7. Listed below are some of the personal characteristics displayed by young people who are successful on their first jobs. Study these carefully and identify your weaknesses.

Perseverance	Good memory
Politeness	Personal cleanliness
Interest	Neatness
Ambition	Respect for authority
Enthusiasm	Patience

8. Does your attitude toward a task, whether it is a school subject, a chore at home, or one of your job responsibilities, influence the effectiveness and efficiency with which you perform that task? Answer the following questions regarding your attitude.
   a. Which school subject or activity do you enjoy most?
   b. Which school subject or activity do you enjoy least?
   c. In which school subject do you make your best grades?
   d. In which school subject do you make your lowest grades?
   e. Describe your attitude when you are preparing for the subjects or activities listed for *a.* and *c.*

9. Listed below are twenty-five negative characteristics that might be found in an inefficient office worker. On a separate sheet of paper, list the positive characteristic which should replace each negative characteristic.

Work Attitudes	Mental Attitudes	Social Attitudes
1. Irresponsible	11. Dishonest	19. Shy
2. Indifferent	12. Inattentive	20. Gloomy
3. Lazy	13. Unperceptive	21. Excitable
4. Unpersistent	14. Inaccurate	22. Discourteous
5. Haphazard	15. Impulsive	23. Tactless
6. Disorderly	16. Fearful	24. Inconsiderate
7. Inflexible	17. Illogical	25. Impatient
8. Dawdling	18. Unimaginative	
9. Shirking		
10. Disloyal		

THE
OFFICE
TEAM

Initiative might be defined as the ability to sense the need to take some action and then take it, without being instructed to do so. Read the following case-incident and rate the initiative of Evelyn Smith, Patricia Hofner, Janis Caldwell, and Jane Wilson. After analyzing the case, rate your own initiative.

EVELYN SMITH IS AN ACCOUNTING AND FILE CLERK FOR THE ACCOUNTing Department of the Stone Mountain Manufacturing Company where she has worked for the past year. She posts charges and payments to the accounts of customers and she maintains the customers' files so that the up-to-the-minute status of any account is always available. She also maintains the accounts payable files. Although the volume of business is such that Evelyn's job is full time, she occasionally catches up and has some extra time. Her job description calls for her to assist with routine tasks such as typing and duplicating when time permits.

This afternoon she completed all the posting and filing on her accounts approximately forty-five minutes before time to go home—five o'clock. She looked around her work station to see if there were any odd jobs she needed to complete. Seeing none, she asked the other two file and accounting clerks in her office, Patricia Hofner and Janis Caldwell, if she could help them. Although neither of them was caught up, they declined because they were sure they would be finished before five. Evelyn was about to relax and take care of some personal business for the rest of the day when Jane Wilson, a purchasing clerk in the Purchasing Department next door, dropped in. Apparently, she was also caught up for the day. She did not seem to be in a hurry, and was eager to relate something to Evelyn. The following conversation took place.

JANE: Boy, Evelyn, you'd better be glad you don't work in the typing pool this afternoon.

EVELYN: Why?

JANE: Carolyn is about to have a fit. The Personnel Department has just given her a ten-page report to have typed, duplicated with fifty copies, stapled, and ready to use in a meeting first thing in the morning.

EVELYN: Well, I don't see the problem. She, Betty, and Louise should certainly be able to do that, if they work together, in forty-five minutes or a little more.

JANE: Yeah, but Betty and Louise are out sick today, and Carolyn is alone. She'll work late tonight!

Being a conscientious worker, with a great deal of initiative and a sense of responsibility and cooperation, Evelyn not only went to the typing pool to help Carolyn get her report out, but she also talked Jane, who is not quite so conscientious, into helping, too.

While she was in the typing pool office, Evelyn's supervisor, Mr. Smith, needed to use the file of one of their best customers, Charder Products, Inc. Evelyn maintains this file, but since she was not at her work station, he asked Patricia to get "the 'Charder' Products account file."

Patricia is a little afraid of Mr. Smith; she was not certain she understood what file Mr. Smith wanted, but she preferred hoping that she could find the right one to asking him to repeat the name. She did not ask Janis to help her because she was afraid she would give the impression she did not understand her work. Therefore, she went to the file to hunt for "Carter Products." After hunting for several minutes in the Accounts Receivable file and not finding it, she finally asked Janis to help her. Janis suggested that she look in the Accounts Payable file. Patricia checked the Accounts Payable file without success. She asked Janis to look. Just as Janis was about to give up looking, Mr. Smith reappeared and asked a little impatiently for the file. The girls explained that they could not find it.

WHAT HAPPENS NEXT?

1. Does Mr. Smith become upset? Does he ask one of the girls to get Evelyn to come and find the Charder file? Does he realize why they cannot find it and spell Charder for them?

2. How do Patricia and Janis feel toward Mr. Smith? Toward Evelyn? Do they become upset with Evelyn because she is not there to get information from the accounts she maintains?

Analysis of Case-Incident

Fact: *Answer the following questions.*

1. What specific actions of the office workers in this case illustrate good initiative? What actions illustrate poor initiative?

2. What other attributes of office workers are illustrated in this case?

3. Is it permissible for office workers to take care of personal business when their work is completed?

Implications: *Indicate which of the following assumptions are valid.*

1. Evelyn is always conscientious about helping her colleagues who are working under pressure.

2. The management of Stone Manufacturing Company motivates its employees to work fast and efficiently by telling them they may take care of personal business when they are caught up with company work.

3. It took a great deal of persuasion from Evelyn to get Jane to go with her to the typing pool to help Carolyn.

4. Carolyn's supervisor should have tried to get some office workers from other offices to help her type and duplicate the report.

5. It is normal for an accounting and file clerk in an Accounting Department to be expected to type and duplicate materials.

6. Evelyn keeps records of transactions and account balances very accurately; she also maintains the accounts files correctly.

7. Management should expect office workers to work late to complete work that must be done.

Verification: *Indicate whether each of the following statements is true, false, or not discussed in the case-incident.*

1. Evelyn was well liked by her peers.

2. Patricia was somewhat afraid of Mr. Smith.

3. Carolyn was behind in her work because she was basically lazy.

4. The ten-page report to be typed and duplicated was primarily statistical in nature.

5. Evelyn usually has free time sometime during the day to take care of personal business.

6. Patricia was confident in her ability to do her work.

7. Patricia always took the initiative when work called for cooperative effort among the workers.

8. Evelyn told Mr. Smith that she was going to the typing pool to help Carolyn with a rush job.

9. Janis is the type of person who does not willingly help anyone else do his work even when she is caught up and has nothing else to do.

Thought: *Be prepared to answer each of the following questions.*

1. Should Carolyn have been given a ten-page report to type, duplicate, and collate forty-five minutes before the end of the work day and told that it had to be ready for use the first thing next morning? Justify your response.

2. What would Evelyn have done if Jane Wilson had not stopped by to tell her "something special?" Is gossiping good or bad? Justify your answer.

3. What can the other girls in the office do to help Patricia overcome her shyness and gain confidence?

4. What is the difference between the duties normally expected of a bookkeeper in a business such as the one described in this case-incident and the duties performed by the accounting and file clerks in this incident?

5. What kinds of machines should workers in the accounting and file clerk position discussed in the case-incident be expected to operate?

Generalization: *Write a statement describing the type of person who could perform successfully in a situation such as the one Evelyn encountered.*

Activities

1. Write a dialogue to portray alternative conclusions to the case-incident if:

    a. Evelyn had merely agreed with Jane that Carolyn would work late that night.

    b. Evelyn had gone to the typing pool alone to help Carolyn get the report done.

    Preface your dialogue with a description of the attitude it portrays. Compare the attitudes displayed in your skits with the attitudes displayed in the actual case-incident.

2. Act out the skits written for Activity One. See if the class can identify the attitudes portrayed.

3. Write the dialogue for role-playing skits to portray positive and/ or negative actions of Mr. Smith, Patricia Hofner, and Janis Caldwell when Mr. Smith asks for the "Charder" account file.

4. Act out the skits written in Activity Three. Have the class write descriptions of the attitudes portrayed by the individuals in each skit.

5. Invite the head of an Accounting Department of a firm in your community to talk to your class about the skills, knowledge, and attitudes needed by office workers in positions similar to the accounting and file clerk position described in this case-incident.

6. Prepare a report on the subject of "How to Overcome Shyness." Present it to the class.

7. Prepare a report on the subject of "Developing Initiative Through Responsible Actions." Present it orally to the class.

8. Prepare a report on the subject of "Making Use of the Full Work Day for the Benefit of the Company." Present it orally to the class.

9. Prepare a report on the subject of "The Grapevine as a Useful Communication Technique in the Office." Present it orally to the class.

BIRTH
OF
A
VOLCANO

Meet Jan Ragan, a receptionist, who must be tactful and use good judgment in working with all types of people both inside and outside the firm. Do you have the kind of personality needed to be a receptionist?

JAN RAGAN HAS BEEN EMPLOYED BY THE P AND Q SAVINGS & LOAN Association as a receptionist for two years. During this time she has consistently greeted callers and her fellow workers with a warm, friendly, and cheerful message. Her work station is located in the front lobby so that all people who come into P and Q must go by her desk. Since the company is small, she operates the switchboard as well as acting as receptionist. People have frequently commented to the president and executive vice-president that they thoroughly enjoy coming to P and Q to do business because they always feel welcome. Jan's smile, twinkling eyes, and her bright "Good morning" or "Good afternoon" always conveys a genuine regard for the person to whom it is directed.

Jan is the type of person who can express warmth and concern without causing people to loiter and talk. She does not gossip and she makes certain that the people who come to her desk receive the proper attention. She is thoroughly familiar with the organizational structure of P and Q, the responsibilities of each department, and the personnel in each department. She is so competent that she has had several offers from other companies in town to work for them as a receptionist, and she has been given several raises. She is capable of doing work demanding greater skills in the office, but P and Q feels that she is more valuable to them as a receptionist. Her supervisor, Mr. Kurtman, recognizes her as a valuable office worker and frequently comments that it was his "lucky day" when Jan Ragan came to work.

In spite of all these good qualities Jan is human, and she occasionally does have problems in dealing with people. Just recently, Miss Smith, who substituted for her so that she could take three breaks during the day, resigned. Renee Cooper, who has been employed for two months at P and Q as a stenographer in the steno pool, was selected to replace her.

Renee is a charming person, an excellent stenographer, and generally she gets along very well with her peers; but she is also ambitious and has few scruples about how she satisfies her ambitions. She is particularly envious of the reputation that Jan has made for herself. Jan had no way of knowing how Renee felt when she was assigned to relieve her for coffee breaks; but she began to feel more and more ill at ease each day when Renee came to relieve her, and she did not know what to do about the situation. She did not want to report Renee's behavior to her supervisor; she was especially upset because she had met someone who did not like her.

On this particular morning Jan had been very busy. There had been a steady stream of calls and callers. In fact, she was so busy with people and calls at the time Renee came to relieve her that she actually had to keep working for five minutes while Renee waited. When she finally was able to break away, Renee flopped down in the seat with the remark, "Some people are just so important, just so busy; it's really too bad no one else can do the work as well as they can."

This remark upset Jan; she lost her composure for the first time since she had been with P and Q and remarked, "That's all right. At least I know how to dress properly. Obviously you don't." With that Jan turned around and left the receptionist work station, feeling stunned. She was relieved because she had expressed her feelings about Renee, but at the same time she felt ashamed about not being able to be friends with her.

WHAT HAPPENS NEXT?

Decide which statement you think best describes what happens next.

1. Jan quickly goes to the lady's lounge where she has a good cry and a cup of coffee. She then relates the incident and the situation, as she sees it, to her supervisor.

2. Jan quickly goes to the lady's lounge where she has a good cry and a cup of coffee. She becomes more upset and rushes back to her work station where she pulls Renee out of the chair and forcefully pushes her away, telling her that she is not to relieve her any more.

3. Renee feels elated about the situation; Jan has reacted exactly the way she had wanted. She rushes off to the supervisor to explain how she has been insulted by Jan.

4. Mr. Kurtman calls both girls into his office and reprimands both of them, makes them apologize to each other, and assures them that if it happens again both of them will be fired.

5. Mr. Kurtman calls each girl into his office one at a time. After listening to both, he realizes that Jan is at fault and fires her.

6. Mr. Kurtman calls each girl into his office one at a time. After listening to both, he decides that someone else should be asked to relieve Jan for her coffee breaks.

Analysis of Case-Incident

Fact: *Answer the following questions.*

1. Which actions taken by the office worker in this case-incident showed good tact and judgment? Which showed lack of tact and poor judgment?

2. What other attributes of office workers are illustrated in this case?

Implications: *Indicate which of the following assumptions are valid.*

1. Jan helped Renee to get her job in the steno pool.

2. Renee enjoyed her work as a stenographer very much.

3. Jan was easy to get along with.

4. Renee was easy to get along with.

5. Jan and Renee made worthwhile contributions to the P and Q Savings & Loan Association.

6. Jan was responsible for many new customers for P and Q.

7. Renee was ambitious.

8. Renee would be as good a receptionist as Jan.

Verification: *Indicate whether each of the following statements is true, false, or not discussed in the case-incident.*

1. Jan, by nature, got along well with people.

2. People enjoyed coming to P and Q to do business.

3. Sometimes Jan took too much time visiting with people.

4. Renee was being groomed by the executive vice-president to take over Jan's job.

5. Jan enjoyed hearing gossip.

6. Jan usually took more than the ten minutes allowed for coffee breaks.

7. Jan had had a particularly rough morning when she lost her self-control with Renee.

Thought: *Be prepared to answer each of the following questions.*

1. How important is the work of the receptionist to a firm?

2. What would you say are the most important qualities needed by a receptionist?

3. Should Jan try to work at her problem with Renee alone?

4. What causes people to needle others as Renee needled Jan in this case?

5. What is the supervisor's responsibility in this case?

6. What happens to the morale of office workers when they work for a long period of time in a situation similar to the one in this case-incident?

Generalization: *Write a statement describing the type of person who could perform successfully in a situation such as the one Jan encountered.*

Activities

1. Select a conclusion which you feel is most appropriate for this case-incident. You might select the same one(s) you selected when you were working on *What Happens Next?*, or you might select a conclusion which is not given. Write a skit that demonstrates the behavior of the persons involved and ask some of your classmates to act it out with you for the rest of the class.

2. What are the responsibilities of the office manager in maintaining harmonious working relationships among the office work-

ers? Where does he go to get help in learning how to do this? Prepare a written report for class presentation. Document your sources of information.

3. What are the most effective means of communications in the office? How can the office manager lessen the possibility of such incidents? Prepare a written and oral report for class presentation. Document your sources of information.

4. Much has been written and said in professional periodicals and professional meetings about the need to involve office workers in the process of making decisions relating to their work and welfare. Do you agree or disagree with this concept of office management? Take a stand and prepare a written report for class presentation. Document your sources of information.

5. It has been said that the morale of office workers is directly related to their productivity: that is, workers with low morale will be low in productivity, while workers with high morale will be high in productivity. Prepare a written report about this topic for class presentation. Document your sources of information.

6. Have you ever tried to rate yourself as a person in terms of how well you get along with other people? Is it important to you what other people think of you? Is it important to you what you think of yourself? Use the following self-evaluation form to take a good look at yourself.

Self-Evaluation Scale

On a separate sheet of paper, rate yourself on each of the characteristics listed. Write down the number of the statement on each scale that best describes how you view yourself.

A. Tact
   1. Exceptionally tactful
   2. Above average in tactfulness
   3. Average in tactfulness
   4. Occasionally tactless
   5. Frequently tactless

B. Consideration
   1. Exceptionally harmonious and considerate of others
   2. Generally more harmonious and considerate than most people

    3. Reasonably harmonious and considerate of others
    4. Sometimes harmonious and considerate of others
    5. Exceptionally hostile and inconsiderate of others

C. Manners
    1. Exceptional manners reflecting ease and grace
    2. Manners better than average, attracting friends
    3. Reasonably well mannered
    4. Sometimes impolite and disrespectful
    5. Exceptionally ill-mannered and crude

D. Judgment
    1. Exceptionally good judgment on most occasions
    2. Better than average judgment on most occasions
    3. Average judgment on most occasions
    4. Tendency to use poor judgment on most occasions
    5. Exceptionally poor judgment on most occasions

E. Loyalty
    1. Exceptionally loyal, can be trusted with strictly confidential matters relating to the success of a project
    2. Generally loyal and faithful in working toward the success of a project
    3. Generally do the work required but make little effort beyond this
    4. Loyalty to a project is sometimes questionable
    5. Generally not loyal to anyone or any project other than self

F. Cooperation
    1. Exceptionally cooperative
    2. Above average in cooperation
    3. Average in cooperation
    4. Sometimes uncooperative
    5. Exceptionally uncooperative

Part II

Relationships with Supervisory Personnel

ALMOST EVERYONE WORKS FOR SOMEONE ELSE. TO A LARGE EXTENT, AN employee's relationship with his supervisor will determine his morale and adjustment to the job. A good relationship will facilitate the employee's acquisition of job skills and good work attitudes. A poor relationship, on the other hand, can prevent an employee from ever making a satisfactory adjustment to his job.

Management recognizes the importance of a good working relationship between an individual employee and his supervisor. Regular performance evaluations are used to encourage communication between them. The supervisor considers both skills and attitudes in these evaluations, which usually become part of the employee's record and the basis for promotions and salary increases.

The successful office worker can encourage the development of a good relationship with his supervisor. He should learn to recognize the limits of his authority, to listen with complete concentration, to follow instructions, and to avoid burdening his supervisor with his personal problems. Supervisors respond well to an employee who is adaptable, courteous, alert, and emotionally stable. Loyalty, discretion, controlled initiative, and pride in the job help cement a good relationship with a supervisor.

Part II will deal with the following conditions and characteristics of office workers: *working under pressure, responsibility, initiative, judgment, willingness to learn, following directions,* and *loyalty.*

THE
COFFEE
BREAKER

Some people feel every office worker should be able to work effectively under pressure. Has Mary Jones adequately prepared herself to work under pressure?

As secretary to Mr. Adam Bigg, vice president for Marvel Production Company, one of Mary Jones' major tasks is to prepare contracts for clients. The contracts state terms for leasing, selling, and maintaining data processing equipment manufactured by Marvel. An excellent typist and proofreader, Mary seldom makes mistakes and never hands a contract on which she has made an error to Mr. Bigg for his signature.

On this particular morning, Mr. Bigg had given her a contract to prepare for an important client, Mr. James Quick, who was arriving shortly on his way out of town to sign the contract. Mr. Bigg wanted the contract to be on his desk when Mr. Quick arrived, although he did not tell her to do this job first. Mary thought she had plenty of time, so she did not prepare the document immediately. Instead, she put it with the other contracts to be prepared while she worked on other assignments. She actually forgot about the urgency of the contract. She even took her coffee break and lingered ten minutes longer than usual. She refilled her coffee cup and took it back to her desk to drink while she continued working as she often did.

When she returned to her desk, there was a note in her typewriter from Mr. Bigg asking about the contract. Fortunately, Mr. Quick had not arrived. Mr. Bigg's note stated that he was going down to another office for a few minutes and that he would pick up the contract on his way back. Mary hurriedly began to prepare the contract. She finished it before Mr. Bigg returned without making any mistakes and rested it on the top of her desk to the right of her typewriter. She had just placed it there and was picking up her cup of coffee when Mr. Bigg came in. In her haste to place the cup down and pick the contract up to give it to Mr. Bigg, she became all thumbs. The coffee cup landed on its side and the coffee spilled onto the contract, the desk, and the floor.

WHAT HAPPENS NEXT?

1. The following statements describe possible reactions that Mr. Bigg might have to the accident. On a separate sheet of paper, rank the statements in order from most desirable to least desirable behavior with "1" representing the most desirable behavior.

   a. Mr. Bigg is furious; he glares at Mary and then, as he goes into his office slamming the door, he yells at her to get the contract typed again immediately.

   b. Mr. Bigg is furious, but he controls his voice and tells Mary to retype the contract and bring it to him as soon as possible. He then returns to his office.

   c. Although Mr. Bigg's face expresses distress that the contract will not be ready, he calmly asks Mary to bring the contract to him when she has finished retyping it.

   d. Mr. Bigg dismisses the incident and calmly asks Mary to bring the contract to him when she has finished retyping it.

   e. Mr. Bigg is furious; he glares at Mary and then yells at her to give him the materials so that he can take them down the hall and ask Mr. Smith's secretary to type the contract.

2. The following statements describe possible reactions that Mary might have to the accident. On a separate sheet of paper, rank the statements in order from most desirable to least desirable behavior with "1" representing the most desirable behavior.

   a. Mary expresses her frustration with a few angry words directed at no one in particular. She ends her tirade with the comment, directed to Mr. Bigg, that she might just as well go home. She suggests he get someone else to type the contract.

   b. Mary is upset, but she controls her voice and tells Mr. Bigg that she will retype the contract and bring it to him as soon as possible.

   c. Mary expresses her frustration with a few angry words directed at no one in particular. She ends her tirade by telling Mr. Bigg that she will retype the contract and bring it to him in just a few minutes.

   d. Although Mary's face expresses distress over the accident, she tells Mr. Bigg that she will retype the contract and bring it to him in just a few minutes.

   e. Mary expresses her distress over the accident, apologizes to Mr. Bigg, and calmly begins to clean up the coffee and to retype the contract.

   f. Mary dismisses the incident and calmly begins to clean up the coffee and to retype the contract.

Analysis of Case-Incident

Fact: *Answer the following questions.*

1. List specific actions which illustrate Mary's reactions to working under pressure. Did she react well or poorly in each case?

2. What other attributes of office workers are illustrated in this case?

3. Would Mary's reaction be influenced by Mr. Bigg's reactions and vice versa? Study each of Mary's reactions in terms of each of Mr. Bigg's reactions. How would the relationship between these two individuals be affected in each case?

Implications: *Indicate which of the following assumptions are valid.*

1. Mary gives no special attention to work her boss tells her should receive priority.

2. Mary is tactful under trying circumstances.

3. Mary abuses company policy about the length of coffee breaks; therefore, she can be expected to abuse other company policies.

4. Having food at one's work station can affect one's efficiency.

5. Mary tends to forget important instructions and needs to devise some scheme to overcome this habit.

6. Office workers of Marvel Production Company may eat and drink at their desks while working.

7. Mary is not a responsible person in the office.

8. Mr. Bigg appreciates the efficiency with which Mary performs her job.

9. Mr. Bigg is difficult to please.

Verification: *Indicate whether each of the following statements is true, false, or not discussed in the case-incident.*

1. Mary placed the completed contract on her desk beside her cup of coffee.

2. Mr. Quick had to wait after his arrival for the contract to be typed.

3. Mary is a very nervous person.

4. Complete accuracy is essential to Mary's work.

5. Mary usually drinks coffee at her desk.

Thought: *Be prepared to answer each of the following questions.*

1. How could Mary's behavior have been modified to avoid this undesirable incident? How could Mr. Bigg's behavior have been modified?

2. Should it be necessary for a business firm to have a policy which restricts personal activities of office workers such as eating, drinking, or smoking while they are on the job?

3. Suppose Mr. Quick had arrived before Mary had begun to work on the contract. How would Mr. Bigg have reacted? How would Mary have reacted? How would Mr. Quick have reacted?

4. Suppose Mr. Quick had arrived as Mary spilled her coffee onto the contract. How would each of them have reacted?

5. Will this incident have any effect on future relations between: Mary and Mr. Bigg? Mary and Mr. Quick? Mr. Bigg and Mr. Quick? Mr. Bigg and his supervisor? Will it have any effect on future promotions of Mary or Mr. Bigg?

Generalization: *Write a statement describing the type of person who could perform successfully in a situation such as the one Mary encountered.*

Activities

1. Bring to class an example (either draw one or copy one from the professional literature) of the placement of materials on and in the secretary's desk. Write a report describing how the proper placement and use of these materials might have prevented this kind of incident from happening.

2. On a separate sheet of paper, indicate whether each of the following statements is true or false.
   a. A secretary's facial expression is a key to her ability to work under pressure in a difficult situation.
   b. A secretary's expression can indicate her physical, mental, or emotional condition.
   c. Whether or not a secretary is tense can be reflected in her facial expression.
   d. A secretary's tone of voice is a key to her ability to work under pressure in a difficult situation.
   e. A secretary's tone of voice can indicate her physical, mental, or emotional condition.
   f. Whether or not a secretary is tense can be reflected in her voice.
   g. The words a secretary chooses to express her feelings are an indication of her ability to work under pressure.
   h. The words a secretary chooses to express her feelings can indicate her physical, mental, or emotional condition.
   i. Whether or not a secretary is tense can be reflected in the words she uses.
   j. A responsible secretary might sometimes take a few extra minutes for a coffee break.
   k. It is better for a secretary to rely on her ability to remember oral instructions than it is for her to indicate a poor memory by writing them down.
   l. A secretary should not give up part of her coffee break nor her lunch period to complete important work.
   m. When a secretary makes mistakes while working under pressure she should blame the circumstances, not herself.
   n. A responsible secretary must demonstrate enthusiasm for her work.
   o. A secretary who tells her supervisor that he should have given an assignment to her sooner if he needed it done quickly is a tactful person.

p. Even though there is a "No Smoking" sign posted prominently in the office, a secretary should smoke until someone tells her specifically that she must not.

q. It is reasonable for a secretary to become sullen when reminded by her supervisor that she has not completed an assigned task.

r. It is reasonable for a secretary to become upset when she encounters a difficult situation that occurs infrequently.

s. It is reasonable for a secretary to have important papers on top of her desk while she is also using the top of her desk for refreshments.

t. It is reasonable for a secretary to express her frustration verbally when she encounters a difficult situation that occurs infrequently.

3. Write an essay to justify your responses to the statements in Activity Two. Cite evidence and document your sources. A discussion of each of the following topics should be included in your essay.

a. Having refreshments at the work station.

b. The importance of facial expressions as well as other bodily movements in human relations.

c. The importance of oral expressions, word usage, and tone of voice in human relations.

d. The importance of mannerisms in human relations.

THE
ABSENTEE

Do you believe that an irresponsible individual can learn to be responsible? How would you rate yourself on this attribute? Read the following case-incident and rate Susan Hays.

SUSAN HAYS HAS BEEN EMPLOYED AS A RECEPTIONIST AND CLERK AT THE Mitchell Pediatric Center for the past four months. Her responsibilities include answering the telephone, making appointments, checking in patients, pulling patient files, stamping the date on the medical record sheet in each file, and taking phone messages for doctors.

Susan is well liked by her fellow workers, the patients, her supervisor, and the pediatricians. The only complaint that Mrs. Banks, Susan's supervisor, has made about Susan is that she is absent too frequently.

For several months, Susan's younger brother, a high school sophomore, has been in trouble with the police about a petty larceny charge. Susan's frequent absences from work have been due largely to her attempts to handle these problems with her brother.

On Saturday morning, Susan called Mrs. Banks, her supervisor, to say that she would not be coming to work. The waiting room was noisy and crowded with incoming patients and visitors. Mrs. Banks was noticeably upset with Susan.

WHAT HAPPENS NEXT?

1. The following statements describe reactions that Mrs. Banks might have to the phone call. On a separate sheet of paper,

rank the statements in order from most desirable to least desirable behavior with "1" representing the most desirable behavior.

   a. Mrs. Banks tells Susan that if she does not report to work she can consider herself fired.

   b. Mrs. Banks screams at Susan, telling her that she is fired, and slams down the phone receiver.

   c. Mrs. Banks quickly explains the situation at the hospital and urges Susan to come to work as quickly as she can get there.

   d. Mrs. Banks reminds Susan of her responsibility to her employer and asks her to report to work as soon as possible.

2. Read the following statements regarding possible actions that Susan might take. On a separate sheet of paper, rank the statements in order from most desirable to least desirable behavior with "1" representing the most desirable behavior.

   a. Susan begins crying and hangs up the phone.

   b. Susan becomes angry with Mrs. Banks and slams down the receiver.

   c. Susan comes to work; she tells the other girl in the office that she feels Mrs. Banks has been unfair with her.

   d. Susan dresses quickly and reports to work.

Analysis of Case-Incident

Fact: *Answer the following questions.*

1. Which of Susan's actions were responsible? Which were not responsible?

2. What other attributes of office workers are illustrated in this case?

3. What is Susan's position at the hospital? What are some of the major tasks that are usually performed by a person in this position?

4. Draw a cartoon to show the conversation that takes place between Susan and Mrs. Banks.

Implications: *Indicate which of the following assumptions are valid.*

1. Mrs. Banks had not previously discussed Susan's absenteeism with her.

2. Susan felt that her family obligations should take priority over her job.

3. Susan was not aware of her responsibilities as a receptionist.

4. Susan and Mrs. Banks had a good working relationship.

Verification: *Indicate whether each of the following statements is true, false, or not discussed in the case-incident.*

1. This was Susan's first absence from her job.

2. Susan had discussed her family problem with Mrs. Banks.

3. Susan had been appointed guardian for her brother.

4. Susan had been employed in this position less than six months.

Thought: *Be prepared to answer each of the following questions.*

1. Under what conditions should an individual's personal life receive priority over her professional life?

2. What policies would you recommend for a company regarding absenteeism?

3. Under what conditions should an employee discuss personal problems with her supervisor? Do you think Susan should have discussed her problem with Mrs. Banks? Why?

4. What personal qualifications would a successful receptionist probably possess?

Generalization: *Write a statement describing the type of person who could perform successfully in a situation such as the one Susan encountered.*

Activities

1. Interview one or more receptionists to determine the tasks they perform. Prepare the questionnaire you will use and have your teacher approve it. Report your findings to the class using either a written, an oral, or a visual format.

2. Interview one or more employers (from one large company and one small company, if possible) to determine company policies regarding absenteeism. Have your teacher approve your interview form. Your class report might be a tape of the interviews, a written report, or an oral report accompanied by visual aids.

3. Invite a receptionist to talk to the class about her duties.

4. Keep a record of absenteeism of class members for one month. Devise a code for recording reasons for absences.

5. Team with another student to prepare a script for a simulated face-to-face or telephone conversation. Tape the conversation. Evaluate your conversations in terms of enunciation and pronunciation of words.

6. With another student, assume the roles of Susan and Mrs. Banks and present an impromptu mini-drama of the incident, including the conclusion of the incident.

GRAPEVINE GOSSIP

As an executive secretary Ann Taylor knows her boss expects her to show initiative in handling various incidents that arise in the office. Read the following selection and decide how you think Ann should handle the problem which arises.

ANN TAYLOR IS AN EXECUTIVE SECRETARY WHO HAS BEEN WITH VIP OIL Company for six years. She has always been a very conscientious and hard-working employee; she was promoted to the top office position in the company. She works directly for Mr. Burke, the president of the company, and works indirectly with all other office personnel. There are fourteen other office workers, including four secretaries in the company. Ann is popular with all the employees, and on many occasions she has been instrumental in eliminating ill feelings, stopping malicious gossip, and working out differences between office employees without a comment to Mr. Burke. Although there is no office manager in the organization, the other employees tend to look upon Ann as their liaison with the top management of the company.

During lunch today Ann overheard some of the girls gossiping. One girl said that she had been told by Mr. Sams, vice-president, that she was to be promoted to a newly created position. One of the other girls replied that she felt the promotion should go to the person with the most seniority (presumably Ann). From past experience, Ann knew that this type of gossip would spread rapidly through the office.

WHAT HAPPENS NEXT?

Read the following actions that Ann might have taken. Decide which response you think is best. Be prepared to justify your choice.

1. Ann normally does not bother her employer with petty gossip, but in this instance she informs him of the incident.

2. Ann reprimands the girl who initiated the gossip, explaining that it could cause misunderstanding and ill feelings and thus damage morale among the office force.

3. Ann ignores the rumor since she feels there is no basis for gossiping to her employer or fellow employees regarding confidential matters of the company.

4. Ann becomes upset because she feels Mr. Burke should have told her about the impending promotion.

5. Ann decides to resign, since she interprets the rumor as an indication that Mr. Burke had lost confidence in her ability to coordinate the office staff.

Analysis of Case-Incident

Fact: *Answer the following questions.*

1. What specific actions of the office workers in this case-incident illustrate good initiative? Which illustrate poor initiative?

2. What other characteristics of office workers are illustrated in this case?

3. List some evidence to support the statement that Ann Taylor was an efficient executive secretary.

Implications: *Indicate which of the following assumptions are valid.*

1. Ann was a loyal, dependable employee.

2. Ann did not gossip.

3. Mr. Burke relied on Ann to handle minor personnel problems among the office employees.

4. Mr. Burke did not have a good working relationship with his employees.

5. The office employees resented Ann because she reported everything that happened in the office to Mr. Burke.

6. Diplomacy is an important trait for any employee.

Verification: *Indicate whether each of the following statements is true, false, or not discussed in the case-incident.*

1. Ann was well liked by other employees.

2. Ann refrained from reporting unimportant incidents and employee gossip to her boss.

3. The rumor originated with a company vice-president.

Thought: *Be prepared to answer each of the following questions.*

1. Where does an office worker's first loyalty belong: to her co-workers, her boss, or the company?

2. How can an employee tactfully avoid petty gossip?

3. It has been said that gossip exists only when there is lack of understanding. Do you agree?

4. Can gossip be curtailed in the office? If so, how?

5. Do you agree that the "grapevine" is a useful tool of administration to convey information unofficially in order to obtain employee reaction to policy? Can you think of an example?

6. What will happen if the employer is not informed of the situation in this case?

7. Should the vice-president have mentioned the new position to one of the girls before it was officially announced to all personnel?

8. Describe the characteristics or traits that an executive secretary should possess.

9. Do you agree with the idea that gossiping is a natural reaction and should be accepted as such and ignored by management?

Generalization: *Write a statement describing the type of person who could perform successfully in a situation such as the one Ann encountered.*

Activities

1. Invite a member of the local chapter of the National Secretaries Association to speak to the class about the duties of an executive secretary and the requirements for becoming a Certified Professional Secretary (CPS).

2. Prepare a report about being an executive secretary as a career. Include training and education requirements, job requirements, and job opportunities. You may want to consult such library sources as the *Occupational Outlook Quarterly,* the *Occupational Outlook Handbook,* and the *Dictionary of Occupational Titles.*

3. Interview an executive secretary. (Prepare your questions in advance. Let your teacher check them.) Tape the interview. Provide class members with a list of your questions to serve as a listening guide.

4. Read the following incidents and formulate answers to the questions following each incident. Be prepared to defend your answers.

   Incident Number 1

   "Have you heard?" Two young secretaries were addressing Cathy Smith, the new secretary to Mr. Baxter.

   "Heard what?" asked Cathy.

   "Well, you know Miss Rich, the bookkeeper, who has been here for 30 years? Sue James in the Sales Department says she heard Miss Rich really tell off the vice-president this morning. It seems that the vice-president was ranting and raving as he usually does on Monday morning. Well, you know how bossy Miss Rich is and how she hates to take criticism from anyone. She really lit into him."

   How should Cathy handle this situation?
   a. Listen eagerly and express genuine interest.
   b. Listen courteously but make no comment.
   c. Stop the storytellers before they have finished and tell them she doesn't want to be a party to gossip.
   d. Report the incident to her boss.

   Incident Number 2

   Jane Davis, who is secretary to Mr. Scott, executive vice-president, was alone in her office, when James Lane returned from a week's vacation. As sales manager, Mr. Lane reported to Mr. Scott.

Jane was surprised to hear Mr. Lane boast of his successful vacation—so successful that he had accepted a new position in the town he had visited. When Jane asked him when he would be leaving, he laughed: "Oh, not for a couple of months yet. I don't intend to give notice here for at least a month. I don't owe the company any more than that."

Should Jane tell her boss of Mr. Lane's plans?

Suppose that Mr. Lane had asked Jane not to tell anyone; would your answer be different then?

Is it part of a secretary's job to keep her boss informed of what goes on in the office?

6. Assume that you are an employee at the Maxwell Company and that you overhear the following conversations. Read each conversation and decide whether each should be considered as gossip and ignored, or reported to the employer or supervisor. Justify your decisions.

Conversation No. 1:

"Did you hear that Mr. Jones, the new Sales Representative, asked Jean for a date on Friday night? Well, I heard Jan and Jim invited them over to their place for the evening."

Conversation No. 2:

"Jo Smith, the new secretary, is not able to get her work done for Mr. Ames because Jane keeps giving Jo her work to do. Mr. Ames probably thinks Jo never does anything. Jo hasn't learned that Jane tries this on every new girl."

Conversation No. 3:

"Did you know that Sue doesn't get back from lunch until 1:30? Jean handles the switchboard during her lunch, and that gives her 30 minutes for lunch while Sue has an hour and a half. Jean doesn't want to get Sue into trouble."

Conversation No. 4:

"Did you know that Margie, the vice-president's wife, calls him at the office at least four or five times during the day? I wonder whom she calls when he is out of town."

Conversation No. 5:

"The salesman with GAB Company was really rude when he called today. He insisted that he had an appointment tomorrow, but that he must see Mr. Jones before he leaves town today."

Conversation No. 6:

"Did you hear Hazel tell Mr. Jones that she was sick yesterday? Sue said she saw her downtown at lunch time. You know how many days she has been out already."

Conversation No. 7:

"I heard Jim tell Mr. Jones that he couldn't finish that report unless he got some help today. I guess Mr. Jones thinks he worked on it yesterday. Too bad he didn't check the golf course around two o'clock."

Conversation No. 8:

"We've called the repairman about this copying machine for three days now. We have to have these copies by tomorrow. I wonder if we could have the company come get this machine? Surely we can get better service than that."

Conversation No. 9:

"Mr. Jones has instructed Miss Smith to get all current matters handled while he is out of the office, but Sue will not do a thing that Miss Smith asks her to do."

Conversation No. 10:

"Did you hear the argument between Jim and Jack this morning? It seems that Jack made some crack about Jim's sales quota and his failure to make it. Anyway, they exchanged some words over it."

THE
TROUBLE
SHOOTER

In this incident you will meet Ben Mitchell, who must exercise sound judgment in reaching a decision. As you read this selection, decide what you would do if you were Ben.

FOR THE PAST TWO YEARS, BEN MITCHELL HAS BEEN A SYSTEMS ANALYST for Superior Electronics Corporation, a large electronics equipment manufacturing firm. After conferring with personnel in operating units, he devises new information-handling workflow sequences. Ben has been with SECO for six years. He joined the company after high school as a coding equipment operator. He learned quickly, and six months later he was promoted to computer and console operator, a position he held for two years. Subsequently, he became a senior systems analyst, responsible only to the manager of the department, Mr. Nelson.

At SECO, Ben has taken advantage of every opportunity for professional training in his field; he participated in numerous company-sponsored training programs and short courses for data processing specialists. Consequently, he has become recognized as an expert in matters related to the development of programs to meet the company's expanding data processing information needs.

This morning Ben is in the process of finalizing the automation of the payroll. This job has to be completed by noon if the company payroll is to be ready at the end of the day.

Mr. Ames, the manager of the Sales Department, has just read the quarterly printout prepared by the Data Processing Department showing a geographic breakdown of sales. He rushed over to see Mr. Nelson, who is out of town. Ames then brushed past the secretary into Ben's office and demanded an explanation for "errors" in the report.

WHAT HAPPENS NEXT?

1. Read each of the four sets of possible reactions by Ben. For each set, write down the response or reaction that was most likely to occur, and the response or reaction that was least likely to occur.

   Set 1

   a. Ben indicates that the report was based on information from the Sales Department and that Mr. Ames should first check his own data.
   b. Ben explains that the report was prepared by an employee currently on vacation and that he will ask someone else to verify the accuracy of the data.
   c. Ben promises to call Mr. Ames' complaint to the attention of Mr. Nelson as soon as he returns to the office.

   Set 2

   a. Ben angrily tells Mr. Ames that he is busy and doesn't have time to talk to him.
   b. Ben refers Mr. Ames to Miss Trimble, who indicates that she is familiar with the report.
   c. Ben replies, "Let's discuss this over a cup of coffee; I need a break from this payroll job anyway."

   Set 3

   a. Ben checks the report and finds that the errors have been made by a programmer. He apologizes to Mr. Ames and assures him that he will request a revised report.
   b. Ben replies, "Now, Ralph, we're all human and prone to make mistakes. We'll check it, and if there's an error, we'll correct it and put out a revised report."
   c. Ben disclaims any knowledge of the report, indicating that Mr. Ames will need to discuss it with Mr. Nelson.

   Set 4

   a. Ben asks the secretary to call the employee who worked on the report to verify the accuracy of the data.
   b. Ben says he knows the report is accurate because he personally worked on it.
   c. Ben explains the urgency of his present payroll task and asks Mr. Ames if they could get together after lunch and go over the report.

2. Read the twelve reactions in the preceding question and select the one that you think is best. Explain your choice.

3. Can you think of actions, other than those listed, which Ben might take?

Analysis of Case-Incident

Fact: *Answer the following questions.*

1. What specific actions taken by the office workers in this case-incident demonstrated good judgment? Which ones demonstrated poor judgment?

2. What other characteristics of office workers are illustrated in this case?

Implications: *Indicate which of the following assumptions are valid.*

1. SECO encourages employees to participate in professional training programs.

2. Mr. Ames is an implusive individual.

3. Ben was accustomed to handling problems in Mr. Nelson's absence.

4. Reports issued by Data Processing for other departments were carefully reviewed by those departments.

5. The urgency of the payroll task took precedence over Mr. Ames' complaint.

6. Ben Mitchell is a personable and even-tempered individual.

7. SECO offers excellent opportunities for advancement in the field of data processing.

Verification: *Indicate whether each of the following statements is true, false, or not discussed in the case-incident.*

1. Ben was recognized as a data processing expert by company employees.

2. When he was away, Mr. Nelson left Ben in charge of the department.

3. Mr. Ames audited all sales reports emanating from SECO.

Thought: *Be prepared to answer each of the following questions.*

1. Do you think SECO would be a good company to work for? Why?

2. Should Mr. Ames have confronted Ben Mitchell with this problem or should he have waited until Mr. Nelson returned?

3. Was Mr. Ames justified in rushing into Ben's office unannounced? Under what conditions, if any, is company management entitled to enter employee offices without advance notice?

4. Was Ben Mitchell's primary responsibility to complete the work on the payroll or to talk with Mr. Ames regarding his complaint?

5. Do you think the conclusion of this incident would have been different if Ben had been a computer operator?

Generalization: *Write a statement describing the type of person who could perform successfully in a situation such as the one Ben encountered.*

Activities

1. Reenact the case-incident, showing how Ben could have handled this problem.

2. Explore career opportunities in the field of data processing; prepare a report and/or a display for the class.

3. Define the following data processing vocabulary words.
   a. input
   b. hardware
   c. print-out
   d. alphanumeric
   e. program
   f. electronic data processing
   g. digital computer
   h. Cobol
   i. binary system
   j. debugging

4. Invite a data processing specialist to talk with the class about job responsibilities and opportunities in the field of business data processing.

5. Visit a data processing installation in a college, technical school, or business.

6. Construct a job ladder identifying jobs in electronic data processing from the simplest to the most complex. You may want to consult the *Occupational Outlook Handbook.*

BUCKING
THE
SYSTEM

Frances Barker is having difficulty adjusting to her employer's procedures for recording certain types of merchandise. Read the following selection to find out what happens when she decides to do it her own way.

FOR THE PAST FOUR MONTHS, FRANCES BARKER HAS BEEN EMPLOYED AS an inventory clerk for Fowler Equipment Company where she is responsible for updating inventory records, compiling inventory descriptions, and revising them. Prior to this time, she had been enrolled at Midland Community College and had worked part-time for Dennard Electric Company in the Accounts Receivable Department.

Recently Fowler Company ordered a copying machine to fill an order from Mathews Electric Supplies. However, before the machine arrived, Mathews Electric decided to purchase another model already in stock. According to company policy, the new machine was to be kept, recorded as open stock, and made available for sale.

Mr. Johnson, the company manager, explained the procedures for handling this situation to Frances. Frances disagreed with Mr. Johnson's manner of handling the transaction and told him she thought it should be handled in another way.

Just then Mr. Johnson was called out of the office on business and Frances completed the transaction as she had suggested, following the procedure that had been in effect at Dennard Electric when she worked there.

A few weeks later, a customer called, requesting a copying machine which he needed immediately. The salesman checked the open stock records but found no machine listed. Since Fowler Equipment Company was unable to supply the needed machine, the sale was lost.

The next day the salesman learned that the company actually did have a copying machine in stock.

WHAT HAPPENS NEXT?

1. Assume you are the salesman; what would you do next?

2. Assume you are Mr. Johnson; what would you do next?

3. Assume you are Frances Barker; what would you do next?

Analysis of Case-Incident

Fact: *Answer the following questions.*
1. What specific action of the office worker in this case-incident illustrates an unwillingness to learn?

2. What other characteristics of office workers are illustrated in this case?

3. What did Frances fail to do in performing the duties of her job?

Implications: *Indicate which of the following assumptions are valid.*
1. Frances failed to follow the instructions given by her employer.

2. Frances was justified in questioning the instructions given by her supervisor.

3. Conformity to company policies is necessary when performing any job within any company.

4. Keeping accurate records is a necessity in the success of any business.

Verification: *Indicate whether each of the following statements is true, false, or not discussed in the case-incident.*
1. Frances had not learned to conform to company policies when she recorded transactions her way.

2. Mr. Johnson encouraged his employees to introduce and try out new ideas.

Thought: *Be prepared to answer each of the following questions.*

1. Why did Frances not follow the directions given her by Mr. Johnson?

2. How should Frances have gone about effecting a new recording procedure if she felt she was right?

3. Does an employee have a right to challenge an established company policy or procedure?

Generalization: *Write a statement describing the kind of person who could perform effectively in a situation such as the one Frances encountered.*

Activities

1. Invite a representative from a large company or organization to discuss company policies in such areas as correspondence manuals where there may be variation from styles most commonly taught in school. (For example, use a representative from a military installation, or a representative from a company using the Administrative Management Society letter style.)

2. Conduct a survey to determine whether employers have special policies regarding the form of accounting entries, filing, correspondence, etc., or whether these are left to the discretion of employees.

3. Prepare a display showing various methods of performing certain job tasks such as filing methods or letter styles.

4. Decide what you would have done if you were Mr. Johnson, the salesman, or Miss Barker. Be prepared to play this role in class.

THE
SECRETARIAL
POOL

*Following directions constitutes one of the most important phases of a
secretary's job. Observe in this incident how a personal distraction causes
Cynthia Bridges to give less than full attention to the task at hand.*

SIX MONTHS AGO, WHEN CYNTHIA BRIDGES WAS EMPLOYED BY HAWK'S,
one of the nation's largest department stores, she was assigned to the ten-
girl secretarial pool. In this position, she took dictation, transcribed it,
and typed other reports.

This job was her first since completing her secretarial training. As a
member of the secretarial pool, she had little opportunity to interact with
other people in the office. Most of her work was channeled to her by her
supervisor, Miss Clayton, who in turn returned it to the officials who had
requested the work. As she began to demonstrate her skills in shorthand
and typewriting, Cynthia was called upon to substitute in taking dictation from several officials and proved herself quite skillful. Recognizing
Cynthia's abilities, executives soon began asking for her more and more.
After approximately three months, it became necessary to assign her to
three buyers permanently.

Cynthia's desk was still located in the secretarial pool. Desks of the
three buyers for whom she worked were connected by buzzer to
Cynthia's desk. They could buzz her; she could not buzz them.

Cynthia became well known among the office and managerial personnel for the speed, accuracy, and neatness with which she took dictation and prepared letters, memos, and other reports. She had little opportunity at this time, however, to perform many of the duties of a
private secretary. For instance, she never had to take calls over the tele-

phone, place telephone calls, or receive callers. She never had the responsibility of scheduling appointments for her bosses. Consequently, during the three months she worked for these three men, she did not have much more interaction with people than she had had before.

Mr. Jonathan Willis' secretary resigned last week. Upon Miss Clayton's recommendation, he employed Cynthia to take her place. Naturally, Cynthia was very pleased with the promotion as well as the added responsibility and prestige. Her desk, well-equipped for secretarial duties, was located in a private office that opened onto a main hall on one side and into Mr. Willis' office on the opposite side. As the head buyer, Mr. Willis had many visitors and telephone conversations during the course of his day. It was his secretary's responsibility to coordinate these activities.

In addition to taking dictation and typing reports, Cynthia received all callers and calls for Mr. Willis. She had to learn her new job well enough so that she could make decisions regarding who should see or talk with Mr. Willis and when. Their telephones had a direct connection so that they could talk with each other privately while either one or both of them has another party on the line.

On this particular morning, Mr. Willis had told Cynthia on his way into his office that he was expecting an important telephone call from Mr. Thomas, the salesman for Ladies Imports, Inc.

Later in the morning when she answered the telephone, a caller identified himself as "Mr. Thomas"—or so she thought. Her attention had been distracted by a young man who walked by her open door just as "Mr. Thomas" was giving his name.

Instead of asking "Mr. Thomas" to hold the line while she checked to see if Mr. Willis was available to talk with him, as she normally did, she connected "Mr. Thomas" directly with Mr. Willis and hung up. Mr. Willis found himself talking not to Mr. Thomas, but to Mr. Thompson, a gentleman with whom Mr. Willis did not wish to talk. Mr. Thompson was trying to sell Mr. Willis a membership in a community country club in which he had absolutely no interest. Mr. Thompson is a persuasive personal friend of Mr. Willis and he could not be told goodbye tactfully and quickly.

WHAT HAPPENS NEXT?

1. Read each of the following sets of Mr. Willis' possible reactions. For each set, write down the response that was most likely to occur and the response that was least likely to occur.

Set 1

a. Mr. Willis buzzes Cynthia's private line and laughingly explains that the caller was Mr. Thompson, not Mr. Thomas whom he was expecting to call.
b. Mr. Willis buzzes Cynthia's private line and tactfully tells her that she should be more careful about putting callers directly on his line. He also explains that she should be careful to get the exact name of his caller, as he points out her mistaking Mr. Thompson for Mr. Thomas.
c. Mr. Willis buzzes Cynthia's private line and abruptly tells her she has made a serious mistake. She has caused him to waste ten minutes of his time with a caller with whom he definitely did not want to talk. Not only that, he also tells her, he is now in a bad mood and the rest of his day will probably be affected by it. He then angrily tells her what she has done.
d. Mr. Willis does nothing.

Set 2

Mr. Willis buzzes Cynthia's private line and asks her to come into his office. When she comes in:
a. He laughingly and tactfully explains what has just happened and tells her how to avoid it in the future.
b. He tactfully and calmly tells her that she should be more careful about putting callers directly on his line. He also explains that she should be careful to get the exact name of his caller. Then he explains what has just happened and tells her how to avoid it in the future.
c. He abruptly tells her what has just happened and how to avoid it in the future.
d. He angrily tells her that she should be more careful about putting callers directly on his line. He also explains that she should be careful to get the exact name of his caller. Then he explains what has just happened and tells her that she must avoid such mistakes in the future.

Set 3

Mr. Willis comes into Cynthia's office, and:

a. His walk, slamming of door, and general manner tell Cynthia he is angry. He loudly and abruptly tells her that she should be more careful about putting callers directly on his line. He also explains that she should be careful to get the exact name of his caller. Then he explains what has just happened and tells her that she must avoid such mistakes in the future.

b. In his usual calm manner he tactfully and calmly tells her that she should be more careful about putting callers directly on his line. He also explains that she should be careful to get the exact name of his caller. Then he explains what has just happened and tells her how to avoid it in the future.

c. He laughingly and tactfully explains what has just happened and tells her how to avoid it in the future.

d. Mr. Willis abruptly asks her if she knows how to use the telephone. He then tells her what has happened.

e. Although he is outwardly calm, he abruptly tells her what has just happened and how to avoid it in the future.

2. The following statements describe possible reactions that Cynthia might have to the incident. On another sheet of paper, rank the statements in order from most desirable to least desirable with "1" representing the most desirable behavior.

a. Cynthia thanks Mr. Willis for calling the mistake to her attention, apologizes, and tells him it will not happen again.

b. Cynthia abruptly tells Mr. Willis that she knows how to use the telephone and that anyone can make a mistake.

c. Cynthia apologizes for the mistake, explains what happened to cause her to make the mistake, and assures Mr. Willis that it will not happen again.

d. Cynthia bursts into tears, blurts out that she just cannot assume so many new responsibilities, and asks to be returned to the secretarial pool.

Analysis of Case-Incident

Fact: *Answer the following questions.*

1. What specific actions of the office worker in this case-incident provide good or bad examples of following directions?

2. What other characteristics of office workers are illustrated in this case?

Implications: *Indicate which of the following assumptions are valid.*

1. Cynthia has a lot to learn about quality performance as a secretary. There is much more to being a secretary than just being skilled in typing and shorthand.

2. Cynthia lets her personal relationships with boys interfere with her work.

3. Cynthia needs more training on the correct use of the telephone in the office.

4. Mr. Willis's confidence in Cynthia's ability and sense of responsibility has been shaken as a result of this incident.

5. Cynthia has not been adequately trained for secretarial work.

Verification: *Indicate whether each of the following statements is true, false, or not discussed in the case-incident.*

1. Cynthia had worked for a number of people while at Hawk's.

2. Cynthia had had many opportunities to interact with people while at Hawk's.

3. Cynthia was well trained in the correct use of the telephone in the office.

4. Cynthia did not feel well on the day the incident occurred.

5. While a member of the secretarial pool, Cynthia placed many calls and received calls and callers as a regular part of her work.

6. Mr. Willis wanted Cynthia for his private secretary even though she had been poorly recommended by Miss Clayton, supervisor of the secretarial pool.

7. Mr. Willis gave Cynthia the wrong name of the salesman from whom he was expecting a call.

8. Cynthia frequently confused people's names.

9. Cynthia should have her hearing checked.

Thought: *Be prepared to answer each of the following questions.*

1. Can a secretary tactfully ask a caller to spell his name so that she can be certain she has it correctly? Is it better for her to be cer-

tain of not embarrassing the caller or herself and hope that she can straighten it out later some other way?

2. If Mr. Willis had been happy to have this chance to talk with Mr. Thompson, should he still say something to Cynthia about her connecting him directly with Mr. Thompson?

3. Suppose Cynthia had buzzed Mr. Willis before connecting him with Mr. Thompson. Would Mr. Willis have caught her error or would he still have had to spend some time on the telephone with the wrong man?

Generalization: *Write a statement describing the type of person who could perform effectively in a situation such as the one Cynthia encountered.*

Activities

1. Invite a speaker from the telephone company to talk to the class about telephone etiquette in the office. You might ask another student to help you select a speaker and make the invitation.

2. Invite an office worker from a large department store to talk to the class about the tasks that are performed by office workers in department stores and the skills and knowledge necessary to perform these tasks.

3. Form a team with some of your classmates and plan a skit of this case-incident, portraying selected conclusions under *What Happens Next?* You may write your skit or plan to do it extemporaneously. Ask your classmates to evaluate your performance and to identify the conclusion you are portraying.

4. Cite some specific techniques that you need to develop in order to improve your ability to listen effectively. You may need to consult library references on listening as an important aspect of communication. Prepare an oral or written report for your class.

BRAND
X
OR
Y?

Just how far does a company expect an employee to go to show his loyalty? This is a problem facing George Carpenter. As you read the following case-incident, place yourself in George's place and see if your actions would be the same.

THREE YEARS AGO GEORGE CARPENTER GRADUATED FROM COLLEGE with a degree in personnel administration. After he graduated he was employed in the Personnel Department of Arlington Automotive Corporation as an interviewer and test technician. George is a personable young man and he is well liked by both management and employees. Two months ago he was promoted to the position of Assistant Personnel Manager. Mr. Irwin, the Personnel Manager, is nearing retirement and he regards George as a prime prospect for the position.

George was married six months ago. Since George's wife works also it became necessary for the couple to purchase another automobile. George shopped for a new car for some time. On Saturday afternoon he and his wife made the purchase, and on Monday morning he drove his new Martin sedan (a major competitor of Arlington) onto the parking lot. A plant security guard spotted the new vehicle and telephoned the information to his superior who, in turn, relayed the news to Mr. Irwin. On the way into the plant, George was kidded by a number of co-workers about his new Martin.

Shortly after he reached his office, Mr. Irwin asked to speak to him. When George entered, Mr. Irwin remarked, "I hear you've bought a new car. What kind did you buy?" George replied that he had thought about it carefully and had finally decided to buy a Martin because the dealer had made him an excellent offer. He had felt that it was important to save as much as he could on the purchase.

Mr. Irwin explained that an employee should be loyal to his employer and that his loyalty should be expressed by supporting the products that the company produces. Driving a competitive automobile tended to suggest to co-workers and to the public a lack of confidence in Arlington and its products. He added that if all employees did this, the company's public relations might be seriously jeopardized. Mr. Irwin felt that the incident was especially serious since George is a member of the Arlington management team.

WHAT HAPPENS NEXT?

1. List as many reasonable choices as you feel Mr. Irwin has in this case. Which choice do you recommend? Why?

2. List the choices you feel George can make now that this incident has occurred. Which do you recommend? Why?

Analysis Of Case-Incident

Fact: *Answer the following questions.*

1. What specific actions of the office worker in this case-incident illustrate loyalty or lack of it?

2. What other characteristics of office workers are illustrated in this case?

Implications: *Indicate which of the following assumptions are valid.*

1. The security guard was acting under orders when he reported George.

2. George was aware of company policy restricting the use of competitive automobiles.

3. Arlington had no company policy governing automobile ownership at managerial levels.

4. George's old car was an Arlington.

5. All Arlington employees drove Arlington automobiles.

6. George was not loyal to Arlington.

Verification. *Indicate whether each of the following statements is true, false, or not discussed in the case-incident.*

1. Arlington employees could receive a discount on new automobiles purchased from the company.

2. Mr. Irwin told George to stop driving the Martin automobile to work.

3. George went to tell Mr. Irwin about the new automobile.

Thought. *Be prepared to answer each of the following questions.*

1. What personal and professional qualities did George Carpenter probably possess that contributed to his success in personnel work?

2. Do you think this incident would have happened if George had been an hourly employee instead of a member of management?

3. Should George's position at Arlington have been a determining factor in his choice of an automobile?

4. Would you be willing to work in a similar office situation? Give your reasons for accepting or refusing such a position.

5. Does a company have a right to prescribe dress or hair style worn by employees?

6. How could you justify a company policy that required employees in managerial positions to drive that company's automobile?

7. Could a company make a similar case against a worker if the competitive product or service were not visible? (For example, should bank employees be required to use the banking services of their employer?) Would the size of community have an influence on the company's policy?

Generalization: *Write a statement describing the type of person who could perform successfully in a situation such as the one George encountered.*

Activities

1. Hold a debate on the topic, "Resolved, A Company Should Expect Its Employees to Use its Products or Services."

2. Survey representatives from several major companies in your community, such as banks, utilities, or automobile dealers, to

determine their policies regarding use of their products or services by their employees.

3. Prepare a job description of a personnel manager. Present your report to the class.

4. Invite a personnel manager to speak to the class about job opportunities and requirements in the personnel field.

5. Write a skit involving a personnel manager and two applicants. One student should act as personnel manager, another student should apply for a position the wrong way, and another student should apply for a position the correct way.

6. What solutions can you offer to the following situation?

   A school has a policy regarding hair length for male students. Three students return in the fall with hair styles not acceptable to the administration. The boys state that they do not enjoy wearing long hair, but that they need to in order to maintain their image for the band. They need the income to stay in school.

7. Vocabulary—Explain the meaning of the following terms as they relate to a job.
   a. loyalty
   b. ambition
   c. tact
   d. attitude
   e. empathy

Part III

Relationships with Individuals Outside the Firm

THE OFFICE WORKER IS CONSTANTLY MAKING PERSONAL CONTACTS WITH people outside the office. The ability to get along with other people easily is therefore one of the distinguishing characteristics of an effective employee. This ability is as important as the technical skills which the job requires.

Although public relations responsibilities are frequently centered in the hands of specialized company personnel, effective public relations is everyone's job. Office workers are in a position which enables them to help create a favorable public image for the firm. Business correspondence, office visits, telephone conversations, and over-the-counter transactions provide opportunities to create good public relations and to make a favorable impact for the organization. These contacts serve as opportunities for the organization to keep its customers, clients, stockholders, government, and the general public informed and to test decisions against public interest and opinion.

Part III focuses on the following conditions and characteristics of office workers which possess potentially important effects in relation to the company's image: *courtesy and responsibility, initiative, tact,* and *willingness to learn.*

DEBITS
AND
CREDITS

Bill Brown enjoys his job as a teller in a bank, even though he sometimes has to deal with people who put him under pressure. Mrs. Calder, one of the bank's best customers, does this in the following situation. Does Bill deal with her effectively?

BILL BROWN HAS BEEN A TELLER FOR THE FIRST COMMERCIAL BANK since he graduated from high school two years ago. Bill's ambition had always been to work in a bank. He is proud of his job: he feels good serving people; he loves the clean, well-kept appearance of his work surroundings; and he enjoys the professional, white-collar feeling of responsibility and importance he gets from dealing with his fellow workers and bank depositors.

His work as a teller normally involves accepting deposits to checking and savings accounts, cashing checks, etc. He is such a friendly person that he works well with people and does an excellent job of studying customers' accounts to find sources of errors. Assisting customers who have problems (real or imaginary) with their accounts has become one of his regular duties.

This morning, Mrs. Henry Calder, a usually pleasant customer, called to speak with the Executive Vice President. She was anything but pleasant. She was blunt and spoke in a loud, highly agitated voice. Since the Executive Vice President and the head teller were out, the receptionist-switchboard operator (Miss Fox) referred her to Bill.

Bill had waited on Mrs. Calder many times in the bank, but he was unprepared for the tirade she delivered when he answered the telephone. She told him that this was not the first time that one of her checks had been returned marked "Insufficient Funds." She was embarrassed; she wanted the Executive Vice President to apologize to her and to the person to whom she had written the check, and she wanted someone to handle her account who would not make mistakes.

Bill could hardly believe that this was the same Mrs. Calder that he had served so many times. When she gave him a chance to speak, he tried to reassure her by explaining that this was an unusual situation and that he was certain they could correct it. She retorted that it did not seem to her to be unusual since the same thing had happened twice in as many months.

Bill then told her that he would check her account on the bank's records and asked her to check her records again to find the error. Mrs. Calder informed him that she had already checked her records and she was positive that the error was on the bank's records; evidently someone else's check had been charged to her account. She had no intention of checking her records again. She added that she was about ready to take her business elsewhere if First Commercial did not start keeping better records. She reminded him that this was the second time that one of her checks had been returned when it should not have been.

WHAT HAPPENS NEXT?

Read the following actions that might have been taken by Bill. On a separate sheet of paper, indicate the response that you think is best. Be prepared to justify your choice.

1. Bill tells Mrs. Calder to take her business elsewhere if she is not satisfied with the service at First Commercial.

2. Bill reminds her that she, not the bank, had made the error the last time she had a check returned for insufficient funds.

3. Bill insists that she check her own records again while he checks the bank records.

4. Bill asks her to bring her records to him so that he can help her check them.

5. Bill tells her that it is possible that the bank has made an error. He asks her to bring her records in so that he can check her records and the bank's records at the same time.

Analysis of Case-Incident

Fact: *Answer the following questions.*

1. What specific actions of the office worker in this case provide

good or bad examples of working under pressure with individuals outside the firm?

2. What other attributes of office workers are illustrated in this case?

3. What activities does Bill Brown perform that are not normally performed by tellers?

Implications: *Indicate which of the following assumptions are valid.*

1. First Commercial makes more than its share of errors on its customers' accounts.

2. Bill is qualified for a much more responsible job than he has.

3. Bill was not concerned about whether or not Mrs. Calder took her business somewhere else.

4. Bill thinks that the customer must be made to feel that the bank believes the customer is always right.

5. Bill was disgusted with Mrs. Calder for calling the bank before completely checking her own records.

Verification: *Indicate whether each of the following statements is true, false, or not discussed in the case-incident.*

1. This was the first time that Mrs. Calder had had a check to be returned for "Insufficient Funds."

2. This was the first time that Mrs. Calder had complained to the bank about how they made so many mistakes.

3. This was the first time that Mrs. Calder had complained to Bill Brown about the errors in her account.

4. Mrs. Calder had checked her records very carefully to see if she had made a mistake.

5. Bill had worked at First Commercial less than a year.

6. Bill had held several jobs prior to working at First Commercial.

7. Normally, Bill got along very well with Mrs. Calder.

Thought: *Be prepared to answer each of the following questions.*

1. Should Bill have kept insisting that Mrs. Calder made the error?

2. Should Bill have told Mrs. Calder that he knew she had made the error the last time instead of the bank?

3. Do you think Bill has the maturity, personality, and reasoning ability to handle this situation effectively? What should be the outcome of this situation?

Generalization: *Write a statement to describe the kind of person who could perform effectively in the situation that Bill encountered.*

Activities

1. Invite one or more bank tellers from banks in your town to talk to your class. A panel discussion might be held. Ask the tellers to relate some of their experiences in dealing with irate customers. Ask them to describe their duties and responsibilities and the skills and knowledge needed to perform them.

2. Check on the possibilities for advancement for persons who start out as bank tellers. What salaries do bank tellers make? You might ask bank officials in your town and/or do research in the library. This might be done in connection with Activity 1. Prepare a report to be presented orally to the class.

3. What kinds of services are provided by banks? You might find answers to this question in some of your texts, in books in the library, or through a survey of the banks in your town. You might use the library to determine the types of banks and the services performed by each, and then find out the specific services rendered by the banks in your community. Prepare a written and oral report for class presentation.

4. What is the Federal Reserve Bank? What is the relationship between banks in your community and the Federal Reserve System? What services does the Federal Reserve Bank provide, and to whom? How are you, as an individual, affected by the Federal Reserve System? Prepare a written and oral report for class presentation. Document your sources of information.

5. What is the Federal Depositors Insurance Corporation? What is the relationship between banks in your community and the Federal Depositors Insurance Corporation? What services does the FDIC provide, and to whom? How are you, as an individual, affected by the FDIC? Prepare a written and oral report for class presentation. Document your sources of information.

6. Write a paper on the applicability of the following statements: "The Customer Is Always Right." To what extent does this statement apply to this case-incident? Is Mrs. Calder right? If not, should she be made to believe that the bank feels she is right? Present your report orally to the class. Document your sources of information.

7. The following scripts may be used for role-playing skits. The skits vary, showing desirable and undesirable conclusions of Bill's telephone conversation with Mrs. Calder. They are written to illustrate the dialogue that might have taken place for each of the alternatives given under *What Happens Next?* Select a skit and act it out with some classmates.

WORKING UNDER PRESSURE

(Three scenes might be created. Mrs. Calder is seated by the telephone in her home. Miss Fox, the receptionist-switchboard operator, is performing her duties near the front entrance of the bank. Bill Brown is at his teller window. As the skit opens Mrs. Calder is dialing and the telephone rings at the receptionist's desk-switchboard.)

(Ring . . . Ring . . .)

MISS FOX: Good morning, First Commercial Bank, Miss Fox speaking. May I help you?

MRS. CALDER: (very emphatically) Yes. This is Mrs. Henry Calder. Can you connect me with the head man at the bank? I want him to straighten out my account.

MISS FOX: Mr. Adams, our Executive Vice President, is not in, Mrs. Calder (questioning tone on the name). You did say "Calder," didn't you?

MRS. CALDER: Yes, I'm Mrs. Calder, C-a-l-d-e-r (she spells it out), and I want to talk with someone who is capable of straightening out my account. I'm tired of getting checks returned for insufficient funds.

MISS FOX: Just a moment, please, Mrs. Calder, I'll see if Mr. Brown can help you.

MRS. CALDER: Mr. Brown? You mean Bill Brown? Now what can he do? He's just a teller.

MISS FOX: He is a teller, Mrs. Calder, but he frequently works with depositors who have problems with their accounts. I think you will find him quite helpful. I'll call him. (Miss Fox dials Bill Brown's number.) (Buzz . . . Buzz)

MR. BROWN: This is Bill Brown. May I help you?

MRS. CALDER: (Still emphatically and increasingly angry) I certainly hope so! I have just received another check marked insufficient funds and I'm tired of the stupid, embarassing mistakes you people make. This is the second time this has happened to me in less than two months. I expect your Mr. Adams to apologize to me and to Mr. William Harpe who had my check returned to him by your bank marked "Insufficient Funds." I am really embarrassed and, to tell you the truth, angry.

MR. BROWN: I understand, Mrs. Calder, and we certainly want to get this straightened out. We're always eager to correct any mistakes that are made. Give me a few minutes to check our records. I'll call you as soon as I've checked them. In the meantime, you might help me by rechecking your records.

MRS. CALDER: (Even angrier) I most certainly will not recheck my records! I have already checked my records, and I have made no mistake. I can add and subtract better than anyone at First Commercial Bank. Don't you have anyone who can do simple bookkeeping? I want someone who is accurate assigned to my account. If you can't do this, I'm going to take my business elsewhere.

WHAT HAPPENS NEXT?

Conclusion 1

MR. BROWN: (Finding it difficult to control himself) Well now, wait just a minute, Mrs. Calder. I think First Commercial Bank would be better off if you did take your business elsewhere. Why don't you just do that?

MRS. CALDER: I will. But, I still want my account straightened out. Goodbye!

MR. BROWN: Goodbye!

Conclusion 2

MR. BROWN: I understand how you feel, Mrs. Calder, and, of course, we don't want to lose you as a customer. I must remind you, however, that the last time one of your checks was returned for insufficient funds, the error was yours, not the bank's. You had made an error in your checkbook in subtraction. Don't you remember?

MRS. CALDER: That's beside the point. I have not made a mistake this time. The bank has, and you had better get it straightened out.

MR. BROWN: Well, let me check your account. Mrs. Calder. It will take me twenty or thirty minutes. I'll call you just as soon as I finish.

MRS. CALDER: Thank you very much. I'll wait. Goodbye.

MR. BROWN: Goobye, Mrs. Calder.

Conclusion 3

MR. BROWN: I understand how you feel, Mrs. Calder, and, of course, we don't want to lose you as a customer. I must remind you, however, that the last time one of your checks was returned for insufficient funds, the error was yours, not the bank's. You had made an error in your checkbook in subtraction. Don't you remember?

MRS. CALDER: That's beside the point. I have not made a mistake this time. The bank has, and you had just better get it straightened out.

MR. BROWN: Be reasonable with us, Mrs. Calder. Our bookkeepers, on the average, don't make more than one error in twelve months. The chances are that the error is yours, and I must insist that you go through your checkbook and bank statements again while I check our records of your account.

MRS. CALDER: I am reasonable, Mr. Brown, but you are giving me no alternative. Your attitude has convinced me that I should take my business elsewhere. But, I still want my account straightened out. Goodbye!

MR. BROWN: Goodbye!

Conclusion 4

MR. BROWN: I understand how you feel, Mrs. Calder, and, of course, we don't want to lose you as a customer. We value your business. Let me suggest this. How about bringing your checkbook and bank statements for the last two months down here so that I can check your records and our records together. Perhaps by looking at both records I can find the problem and make suggestions that will be helpful to both of us. It is possible that we have made an error here, but I can find it more easily if we have your records, too.

MRS. CALDER: Well, if you think my bringing them down there will be helpful to you in straightening out your records I'll be glad to do so.

MR. BROWN: I believe it will, Mrs. Calder, and I certainly do appreciate your willingness to help us out this way.

MRS. CALDER: You're very welcome, Mr. Brown. When would you like me to bring them?

MR. BROWN: Well, how about ten o'clock in the morning?

MRS. CALDER: That's fine. And thank you, Mr. Brown. I'll see you in the morning. Goodbye.

MR. BROWN: Goodbye, Mrs. Calder.

Conclusion 5

MR. BROWN: I understand how you feel, Mrs. Calder, and, of course, we don't want to lose you as a customer. Let me make this suggestion. How about bringing your checkbook and bank statements for the last two months down here so that I can check your records.

MRS. CALDER: But, I'm certain there is no error in my records, Mr. Brown.

MR. BROWN: Perhaps not, but it will be helpful to me if I can compare what you have with what we have. I think I can get to the source of the difficulty much sooner if you can bring your records.

MRS. CALDER: Well, I'm just so busy; but, if you really think it will help you find your error, I guess I can bring in my records. Would tomorrow morning be all right?

MR. BROWN: Yes. How about ten o'clock?

MRS. CALDER: That's fine. I'll see you then. Now, did you say the last two bank statements, cancelled checks, and my checkbook?

MR. BROWN: Yes, Mrs. Calder, and thank you very much for being so cooperative.

MRS. CALDER: You're very welcome, Mr. Brown. See you in the morning.

MR. BROWN: Goodbye, Mrs. Calder.

THE
RECEPTIONIST

The secretary-receptionist's job demands responsibility. As you read and analyze the following case-incident about Jane Black, make a list of her responsibilities.

JANE BLACK HAS BEEN A SECRETARY-RECEPTIONIST IN THE RESEARCH DE-partment of the Rheem Paper Company for eighteen months. Prior to this time, she had been employed by a large insurance company as a typist, working in an office with twenty other girls. Her current duties include greeting callers, operating the switchboard for the department, and typing for several members of the department.

This morning Jane received few outside calls and no visitors; she has been busy typing a statistical report that the department head needs for an afternoon meeting. While she was engrossed in her typing, a visitor came into the reception room without her seeing him. After waiting for approximately ten minutes as Jane typed, he finally became offended and noisily began to leave the room.

WHAT HAPPENS NEXT?

Read the following statements describing possible actions that Jane might take. Then rank the statements on a separate piece of paper from most desirable to least desirable behavior.

    1. Jane raises her head toward the visitor, completes the line on which she is typing, and asks the visitor if she might help him.

2. Jane ignores the visitor, although she sees and hears him. She decides that she has too much work to do and that getting the report typed is more important than greeting the visitor.

3. Jane raises her head toward the visitor, completes the line on which she is typing, mumbles to the visitor that she simply has too much work to do, and grudgingly asks him if she might help him.

4. Janes stops typing, apologizes for being so engrossed that she had not noticed the visitor, and asks if she might help him.

5. Jane quickly gets up from her typewriter, moves toward the visitor, apologizes for not having noticed him, and asks if she might help him.

Analysis of Case-Incident

Fact: *Answer the following questions.*

1. What specific actions of the office worker in this case provide good or bad examples of assuming responsibility in dealing with individuals outside the firm?

2. What other attributes of office workers are illustrated in this case?

3. What are Jane's duties? Which of her tasks should have priority?

Implications: *Indicate which of the following assumptions are valid.*

1. Jane gave the most attention to the responsibility she thought was more important at the time.

2. It was essential for Jane to perform all assigned duties with equal attention to all.

3. Jane knew the visitor was there but wanted to get her report done.

4. The visitor was not accustomed to being ignored.

5. Jane showed discourtesy in not receiving the visitor properly.

6. The visitor's attitude toward the firm was not favorable after the incident.

7. At a glance Jane did not recognize the visitor; she decided he was unimportant and ignored him.

Verification: *Indicate whether each of the following statements below is true, false, or not discussed in the case-incident.*

1. Jane usually does not overlook visitors as they enter the office.

2. Jane has more tasks to perform than should be expected of one office worker.

3. Jane has had more than the usual number of callers on the day of this incident.

4. Jane is an experienced office worker.

Thought: *Be prepared to answer each of the following questions.*

1. How could this undesirable incident have been avoided?

2. What personal qualifications will make a secretary successful in greeting callers? What cautions should she observe?

3. Is there any indication that Jane lacked the qualities necessary in performing the duties of secretary-receptionist?

4. Should all callers be treated with the same degree of courtesy? Is appearance a good basis for judging whether a caller is welcome?

5. How can patience and self-control be used in similar incidents?

6. If Jane had recognized the visitor as he was leaving, what could she have done to follow up the incident?

7. In what way is a secretary a public relations representative for her employer?

8. Could certain office modifications help to avoid similar incidents in the future?

9. Should the incident have been reported to Jane's employer?

10. Should the blame ever be put on the visitor?

Generalization: *Write a statement to describe the kind of person who could perform successfully in the kind of situation Jane encountered.*

Activities

1. With other students, write a short skit for this incident with several different endings, and present it to the class.

2. Draw an office arrangement that might cause the kind of situation described in this case-incident; then draw an office arrangement that might prevent this type of incident from happening. You might want to consult some textbooks showing office layouts.

3. On a separate sheet of paper, indicate whether each attribute listed is desirable and essential for successful performance by a secretary-receptionist.
   a. Graciously makes all visitors feel they are guests.
   b. Always groomed to undergo scrutiny.
   c. Sometimes depressed and moody.
   d. Poised when dealing with unfamiliar situations.
   e. Tactful at all times.
   f. Prone to make snap judgments.
   g. Tastefully keeps the reception center attractive.
   h. Constructively busy at all times.
   i. Exchanges confidental information with visitors and co-workers.
   j. Loyal to her employer.
   k. Gives preferential treatment to certain visitors.
   l. Willing to listen patiently to another's point of view.
   m. Represents the company with a friendly smile.
   n. Displays a pleasant and businesslike attitude.
   o. Makes unidentified callers wait several minutes.
   p. Displays a cordial, impersonal interest in visitors and callers.
   q. Considers it her responsibility to entertain all visitors.
   r. Courteously treats all visitors the same.
   s. Displays confidence when handling her job.
   t. Displays responsibility by accepting and admitting errors rather than making excuses for them.

THE
PLANT
TOUR

What would you do if you were caught in a completely new situation, one that you felt you knew absolutely nothing about? This happened to Rebekah Fowler, and it is not unusual for office workers to find themselves in such situations.

REBEKAH FOWLER HAS WORKED FOR COASTAL TELEPHONE COMPANY for over five years, since she graduated from high school. A bright girl, she has made steady progress, receiving promotions and increased responsibility. She is now in charge of training workers to be marketing representatives in the Customer Services Department. Her work station is located in the center of the Customer Service Office where there are twenty-eight marketing representatives, four supervisors, an assistant manager, and a manager. They are responsible for maintaining customer accounts, processing all requests for customer service, and handling complaints.

Rebekah conducts a three-month training period for each newly employed worker in Customer Service. Much of the training consists of individualized instruction monitored by remote electronic training devices. In addition, Rebekah assigns various individuals to work with the new employee. Rebekah uses this opportunity to observe more experienced workers; she is thus able to upgrade their performance by advising them of more efficient practices she has observed and by teaching them to overcome poor practices.

She occupies a staff position in the office with no direct authority or responsibility relationships with the twenty-eight workers and their supervisors. However, because of the informal relationships and rapport she has developed, she is generally looked upon as third in command by the twenty-eight workers and their supervisors, ranking below only the manager and assistant manager.

Two weeks ago Dr. James White, an office management professor at the local state university, requested that his management class be allowed to tour the office facilities. Mr. Scott, the manager of Customer Service, was asked to conduct the tour; he made arrangements with all departments for someone in each to be responsible for giving an explanation of the work done there. It was necessary for the tour to begin at 11:05 A.M. and to end promptly at 11:55 A.M., so that the students could attend their classes before and after the tour.

In the meantime, Mr. Scott found that he would have to be out of town on the morning of the tour, and he asked the assistant manager of Customer Service, Mr. Sasser, to take the class through the facilities. All arrangements were made and Doctor White's class had been told that Mr. Sasser would meet them promptly at 11:05 in the hall at the main entrance to the building.

Rebekah did not even know that there was to be a tour. At 11:10 A.M. she received a telephone call from Lou Dorcets, the receptionist.

REBEKAH: Customer Service, Miss Fowler speaking.

LOU: Rebekah, Doctor White is here with his class from State. Mr. Sasser was supposed to meet him at 11:05.

REBEKAH: There must be some mistake; Mr. Sasser is in conference.

LOU: Well, there are about twenty people in this hall down here waiting for him, and Doctor White appears to be getting a little nervous.

REBEKAH: Well, I don't know what to do, and Mr. Sasser is in President Morgan's office. I wouldn't dare interrupt them. Mr. Morgan gave specific orders that they were not to be disturbed for any reason; there must be some kind of emergency.

LOU: Well, I'll tell Doctor White someone will be right down. Goodbye.

WHAT HAPPENS NEXT?

1. The following statements describe possible actions that Rebekah might take. On a separate sheet of paper, rank the actions in order from most desirable to least desirable, with "1" representing the most desirable action.
   a. Rebekah panics and does absolutely nothing, leaving Doctor White and his office management class waiting in the hall.

b. Rebekah panics and begins calling all the supervisors and workers in the office and asking them what she should do.

c. Rebekah panics and feels this is one time she must take a chance on interrupting Mr. Morgan and Mr. Sasser.

d. Rebekah calmly and quietly thinks over the situation and quickly constructs in her mind what the tour is. She calls department heads to see if they are alerted to the tour. Finding that they are, she turns her trainee over to a worker, lets the supervisors know where she will be, and goes down to meet Doctor White's group.

e. Rebekah immediately tells one of the supervisors that she is going down to meet Doctor White's class; asks her to tell the other supervisors, and to alert the department heads that she will be taking the class through while Mr. Sasser is in conference with Mr. Morgan.

2. The following statements describe possible reactions that Doctor White and his students might have. Rank the actions in order from most desirable to least desirable, with "1" representing the most desirable action.

a. At 11:15 Doctor White becomes furious; in front of his class he berates the receptionist, and tells her he insists on talking to the president or whoever is in charge of the office—if anyone is. Some of his students become embarrassed; some of them enjoy the tirade. Some of them tell him he has taken them on a wild goose chase.

b. At 11:15 Doctor White calmly explains to the receptionist that the tour is on a strict schedule because of the students' classes and asks her to see if she can try again to see what the situation is. In the meantime, he and the students are admiring the entry way, the reception room, and the teller's cage where customers pay bills. They quietly discuss such things as the door, color, lighting, carpeting, furniture, equipment, and layout in terms of the principles discussed in class. They also unobtrusively observe the way the receptionist performs her duties.

c. At 11:20 Doctor White gathers the class together and tells them that there is some problem; he asks them if they would like to wait a few more minutes to see if they could go through some of the offices or if they would like for him to try to arrange another day to come back to Coastal? They decide to wait.

d. At 11:20 Doctor White apologizes to his class for bringing them on a wild goose chase and tells them the tour is off and that he shall certainly not bring another class to Coastal. He also says he will write a nasty letter to the president of the company.

Analysis of Case-Incident

Fact: *Answer the following questions.*

1. What specific actions of the office workers in this case provide good or bad examples of initiative in dealing with individuals outside the firm?
2. What other attributes of office workers are illustrated in this case?

Implications: *Indicate whether each of the following assumptions is valid.*

1. Rebekah Fowler was a better teacher of marketing representatives than she was a marketing representative herself.
2. The twenty-eight marketing representatives and their four supervisors in the Customer Services Department were responsible to Rebekah, who in turn was responsible to the assistant office manager.
3. Rebekah is well liked by her co-workers in the Customer Services Department.
4. Rebekah was frequently called upon to take over for Mr. Sasser and Mr. Scott.
5. Mr. Scott and Doctor White had been very careful to plan a meaningful tour of the Coastal Telephone Company offices for the office management class.
6. Rebekah was able to give the office management class a tour that would reinforce some of the learnings they had accomplished in the classroom.
7. When Rebekah greeted Doctor White and the students, she began the tour with an apology for being so late, carefully placing blame for the mix-up on Mr. Sasser and Mr. Scott.

Verification: *Indicate whether each of the following statements is true, false, or not discussed in the case-incident.*

1. Rebekah has really been working at Coastal for too short a time to manage her responsibilities well.

2. Dr. White and his students were prompt in arriving for the tour.

3. Mr. Sasser asked Rebekah to be ready to take the class on tour if he was not back from the president's office.

4. Coastal Telephone was always delighted to show groups through its facilities.

Thought: *Be prepared to answer each of the following questions.*

1. Why do companies provide guided tours of their facilities to civic and educational groups?

2. Do you think Rebekah should have felt responsible for taking the class on tour? Do you think you would have, if caught in a similar situation?

3. What did Doctor White expect to accomplish by taking his class on a tour of Coastal Telephone offices?

4. Was it Rebekah's responsibility to check on the tour for Doctor White any more than it was Lou's responsibility? Did Lou act responsibly?

5. What is the public relation role of the Customer Services Department?

Generalization: *Write a statement describing the type of person who could perform successfully in a situation such as the one Rebekah encountered.*

Activities

1. Draw an organizational chart showing the authority and responsibility relationships among personnel in the Customer Services Department.

2. Describe, in paragraph form, the vertical-horizontal relationships among the personnel in the Customer Services Department. You may want to use the organizational chart prepared for Activity One as a guide.

3. Draw an office layout showing a possible arrangement of work stations in the Customer Services Department. Assume that all thirty-five workers are in one large office.

4. Assume the Customer Services Department is to be remodeled in terms of the latest concept of office landscaping. Write a paper making suggestions of possible considerations. Library research as well as a survey of some office equipment should provide ideas. Document your sources.

5. It has been said that every employee in a business firm plays a role in shaping the public image of a firm. Write a paper explaining this theory; if possible, include some quotations from current periodicals that discuss the theory. Relate what you write to the situation described in this case-incident. Document your sources. How does each employee in this firm have a role in shaping the public's image of the firm in this situation?

6. What kinds of office jobs are available with telephone companies? What are the qualifications for each? What are the prevailing salaries? What are the possibilities for promotion? Prepare a written and oral report for class presentation. Document your sources.

7. Prepare a written and oral report for class presentation on the characteristics of the environment of a well-planned reception room. Include a discussion of layout, color, lighting, air conditioning, noise, equipment, furniture, and landscaping. Document your sources.

THE PHILANTHROPIST

In this case-incident you will meet Phyllis Drew who, as an administrative assistant, daily faces situations which require tact. As you read this selection, decide whether you could remain calm if you were Phyllis.

MRS. PHYLLIS DREW IS ADMINISTRATIVE ASSISTANT TO DR. ROBERT Glenn, president of Westover College, a small private liberal arts institution enrolling approximately 1,000 students. Phyllis is a college graduate with a degree in Office Administration. She had had several years experience as a secretary before being promoted to her present position a year ago.

Phyllis deals effectively with students, parents, and visitors to the college. On many occasions she has handled problems with disgruntled students, has consoled uneasy parents of first-quarter freshmen, and has talked with visitors to the college.

One of Phyllis' responsibilities is to schedule appointments for Dr. Glenn and see that he is on hand to keep them. Dr. Glenn has a habit of forgetting appointments when he becomes involved in an activity he feels is more important to the college. Often he forgets to tell Phyllis where she may reach him when he leaves the college office.

This morning Phyllis reminded Dr. Glenn of his ten o'clock appointment with Mr. Millstead, a wealthy local resident well known for his financial support to education. In an earlier conversation, Mr. Millstead had implied to Phyllis that he was considering the establishment of several scholarships at Westover for economically handicapped students.

At 9 A.M. Dr. Glenn walked out of his office and told Phyllis that he would be back in about fifteen minutes. "Don't forget your ten o'clock appointment with Mr. Millstead," she called as he was leaving.

"I'll be back in plenty of time," he replied.

Promptly at ten o'clock Mr. Millstead arrived for his appointment with Dr. Glenn, who had not yet returned to his office. Phyllis asked Mr. Millstead to be seated, explaining that Dr. Glenn was expecting him but had been detained; she added that he would return momentarily. She offered him current reading materials as well as brochures describing the college, its program, and activities.

Fifteen minutes passed and Dr. Glenn had not returned. Phyllis noticed that Mr. Millstead was becoming restless, and frequently glanced at his watch. Fifteen more minutes elapsed and Dr. Glenn still had not returned.

WHAT HAPPENS NEXT?

1. Select the statement (or write one) that you feel best describes Mr. Millstead's reaction.
   a. Mr. Millstead, obviously annoyed, storms out of the office without saying a word.
   b. Mr. Millstead states that he is not waiting another minute for a person who obviously does not want his financial support for the college.
   c. Mr. Millstead tells Phyllis that he has another appointment and will have to leave now.
   d. Mr. Millstead tells Phyllis to tell Dr. Glenn to call his office for an appointment if and when he wants to see him.
   e. Mr. Millstead tells Phyllis that he has a very busy schedule and asks her to try to locate Dr. Glenn.
   f. Mr. Millstead says he is sorry he missed Dr. Glenn and perhaps they can get together some other time.

2. Select the statement (or write one) that you feel best describes Phyllis Drew's reactions to Mr. Millstead.
   a. Phyllis excuses herself, goes into Dr. Glenn's office, and tries to locate him by phone.
   b. Phyllis explains to Mr. Millstead that she is certain an emergency has arisen and that she will try to locate Dr. Glenn by phone.
   c. Phyllis states that she is sorry that Dr. Glenn has not kept the appointment, but that she cannot help it.
   d. Phyllis apologizes to Mr. Millstead for the inconvenience caused him and assures him that Dr. Glenn will call him as soon as he returns to his office.

e. Phyllis asks Mr. Millstead if he would like to make another appointment.

f. Phyllis explodes and says that either Dr. Glenn will have to start keeping his appointments or she will quit.

Analysis of Case-Incident

Fact: *Answer the following questions.*

1. What specific actions of the office worker in this case provide good or poor examples of using tact in dealing with individuals outside the firm?

2. What other attributes of office workers are illustrated in this case?

3. List some of the tasks performed by Phyllis as an administrative assistant that would not normally be done by a secretary.

Implications: *Indicate which of the following assumptions are valid.*

1. Dr. Glenn was usually on time for appointments.

2. Phyllis often had to cover for Dr. Glenn when he was late for appointments.

3. Phyllis was a personal friend of Mr. Millstead.

4. One of Phyllis' jobs was to solicit financial assistance for the college.

5. Phyllis was unhappy in her present position.

6. Mr. Millstead was an important man who did not like to be kept waiting.

7. Mr. Millstead did not make a financial contribution to the college.

Verification: *Indicate whether each of the following statements is true, false, or not discussed in the case-incident.*

1. A portion of Phyllis' duties dealt with public relations.

2. Phyllis was able to justify Dr. Glenn's absence to Mr. Millstead.

3. Dr. Glenn was well liked by the faculty, students, and alumni of Westover College.

Thought: *Be prepared to answer each of the following questions.*

1. What unbusinesslike qualities did Dr. Glenn display?

2. What is an employee's responsibility when the employer or supervisor is late for an appointment?

3. What are the effects of tardiness for appointments on public relations?

4. What positive qualifications did Phyllis display in this incident?

5. Under what conditions, if any, would an employer be justified in telling a customer or visitor or fellow worker that she did not know where her boss was or when he would return?

6. Would you be willing to work in Phyllis' job? Give your reasons for accepting or rejecting her position.

Generalization: *Write a statement describing the type of person who could perform effectively in a situation such as the one Phyllis encountered.*

Activities

1. Write to several colleges, or examine college catalogues to (1) see if a degree is offered in Office Administration or Secretarial Science, and (2) determine the courses required for the degree. Present your findings to your class.

2. Write and enact a skit based on this incident in which Dr. Glenn returns at 10:30 A.M.

3. Select one characteristic or trait that is desirable for an office worker. Write an incident in which this characteristic is demonstrated by a worker.

4. Arrange a model desk illustrating the items that Phyllis would need in her position as administrative assistant.

5. Quick judgments are sometimes made without knowing all the facts of the case. Make a list of negative statements made by you to others. Opposite the statements, write what you believe may have caused you to be negative. See if you can find a reason other than your dislike for them.

6. For one day, list the irritating things done in business or at school by one member of the opposite sex.

7. For one day, list the irritating things done in business or at school by a member of the same sex.

8. Compare the two lists. Which sex tends to irritate you more? Do you think you may be doing something to bring out the worst in people? What are some of the things you do that might irritate women or men?

9. For one day, casually express appreciation for everything that is done for you. If anyone opens a door, or helps you in any way, say "Thank you," and smile. Report to the class whether it made your day more pleasant.

10. Have you ever lost your temper or in any other way lost control of your emotions in a working situation? If so, what was the result? Do you see any other way you could have handled the situation? Explain.

11. This week, every time a person says anything to you of a complimentary nature, say, "Thank you." Describe the results.

12. This week, casually compliment five of your co-workers or classmates. Keep your words and tone casual; do not be sarcastic.

13. For one week, keep a record of your moods. Each night before you retire, write down which of the following phrases best described your mood that day:

    Very happy
    Moderately happy
    Neither happy nor depressed
    Somewhat depressed
    Very depressed

    At the end of the week, see if you need to work on your emotional habit patterns.

14. Deliberately choose the most difficult person you know, and begin a campaign to improve your relationship with him or her. Once a week, write the extent of progress you have made in a log. Be sure to date each progress report.

THE UNEXPECTED CALLER

Most companies give newly employed workers, particularly those at the management level, an orientation to the company so that they will have a better understanding of their role in the company with respect to the roles of all other workers. The situation in this case-incident points up how a willingness to learn the relationship of one's job to all other jobs in the company is important to public relations as well as individual progress.

GWENDOLYN THATCHER HAS BEEN EMPLOYED AS SECRETARY TO MR. C. N. Southern, president of Southern Manufacturing, for about four weeks. Prior to this time, she had worked for three months in the company stenograph pool. In this capacity, she worked for various executives, including Mr. Southern. The executives had all been impressed with her ability to produce quality work quickly, efficiently, and cheerfully. Although she had been with the company only a short time and this was her first job, Mr. Southern and the other executives were so impressed with her ability, her personal bearing and attitude, her interest in her work, and her desire to gain a broad understanding of the company that she was made his private secretary.

Although Gwen is certified to teach business education at the secondary school level, she really does not know whether she wants to teach or to work as a secretary. With the encouragement of her instructors at the university, who have emphasized the importance of practical work experience for vocational office occupations teachers, she decided to get some work experience before teaching. When she applied for a position as secretary with Southern, she was not at all satisfied with the position in the stenograph pool which was offered her; she decided to take it, however, because this was the kind of job that most vocational office training students whom she might teach would hold upon the completion of their educational program. Her experiences at Southern have thus far been very good. She has worked hard, demonstrated a willingness to learn about the company, and received appreciation for her efforts from her supervisors.

All the officers and management personnel of the company, including the business manager, left early this morning to attend a one-day conference planned for manufacturers of fabrics for mens' clothing. Southern Manufacturing Company is one of the leading manufacturers of such fabrics in this section of the country. The purpose of the meeting is to introduce manufacturers to a new synthetic fiber that has just been invented; the company manufacturing it claims it will revolutionize mens' clothing by eliminating the need for dry cleaning. The officers will discuss all aspects of using this fiber in manufacturing fabrics. Since the conference will last only one day, and since no one had any major appointment for the day, Mr. Southern felt it important enough for all management personnel to attend. Actually, no one was left in charge, except departmental supervisors and foremen in charge of their particular workers. So little had been said about this meeting that very few workers knew that all management personnel were away from the plant. In fact, Mr. Southern casually told Gwen as he left to take care of things while he was away, without mentioning who was going. He did explain why and where he was going.

At ten o'clock, Gwen received a call from Janice, the receptionist, that Mr. Caleb Watrous, president of El Captain Manufacturing Company of Mexico in Mexico City, was asking to see Mr. Southern. By this time, all the office workers realized that no officers or other management personnel were around. Gwen told Jan to send him to her office so that she could talk with him.

Gwen did not know that Mr. Watrous was in the United States for two reasons; he was a tourist who was combining business with pleasure. He was investigating manufacturing firms who might possibly provide new sources of fabrics for the mens' suits he manufactures in Mexico City. Since he was on a pleasure trip as well as a business trip, he felt no sense of urgency and made no plans for specific appointments.

WHAT HAPPENS NEXT?

Choose the statement that you think best describes what Gwen does.

  1. Gwen apologizes about the absence of Mr. Southern and the other officers and asks Mr. Watrous for his address so that she can have Mr. Southern write to him.

2. Gwen apologizes about the absence of Mr. Southern and the other officers and asks Mr. Watrous if he can return tomorrow when Mr. Southern can be here.

3. Gwen explains the absence of Mr. Southern and the other officers to Mr. Watrous and asks Mr. Watrous for his address so that she can have Mr. Southern write to him.

4. Gwen explains the absence of Mr. Southern and the other officers to Mr. Watrous and asks Mr. Watrous if he can return tomorrow when Mr. Southern can be here.

5. Gwen explains the absence of Mr. Southern and the other officers to Mr. Watrous. With tactful questions she learns enough from Mr. Watrous to know who he is, what he is doing in the United States, and what his particular interest is in visiting Southern Manufacturing Company. She proceeds to give him specific information about the company, its history, equipment, facilities, personnel, capabilities, volume of business. She then takes him to the foremen, supervisors, and some of the workers at their work stations. She explains some of the processes and has some of the workers describe to Mr. Watrous what they are doing.

Analysis of Case-Incident

Fact: *Answer the following questions.*

1. What specific actions of the worker in this case provide good or bad examples of willingness to learn how to deal with individuals outside the firm?

2. What other attributes of office workers are illustrated in this case?

Implications: *Indicate which of the following assumptions are valid.*

1. It is unusual for a secretary of the president of a firm to take the responsibility of showing a prospective client through the firm.

2. It is common practice for all the officers and management personnel of a firm to be away at the same time.

3. All workers at Southern Manufacturing Company were well versed in the nature and scope of the company's activities and their place in the company.

4. Gwen will take a position as a teacher in the local public secondary schools after another year as Mr. Southern's secretary.

5. Gwen learned to like her work as a secretary at Southern very much.

Verification: *Indicate whether each of the following statements is true, false, or not discussed in the case-incident.*

1. The workers at Southern had been well informed about who was in charge while the officers and management personnel were away.

2. Gwendolyn Thatcher was well liked by her co-workers.

3. Gwen knew exactly what she wanted to do following her graduation from the university.

4. Gwen had held many jobs prior to beginning her work at Southern.

5. Gwen advanced rapidly at Southern for reasons other than her performance, knowledge, skills, and attitudes as a secretary.

Thought: *Be prepared to answer each of the following questions.*

1. Should Mr. Southern have left at least one officer or member of management in charge of the firm while the others were at the meeting in Atlanta?

2. Would you view this company as a progressive, growing, developing company? Explain your response.

3. What qualities do you feel Gwen has which helped her to advance so rapidly from the secretary-clerk-stenographer position to that of secretary to the president?

4. What would be the best conclusion to this case-incident?

Generalization: *Write a statement describing the type of person who could perform effectively in a situation such as the one Gwen encountered.*

Activities

1. Write a paper for presentation to the class outlining the duties, responsibilities, and qualifications of secretaries to the presi-

dents of firms. You should seek information from your library, and you might want to interview some secretaries in your community who hold such positions. Document your sources.

2. What kind of education best prepares a person for a top-flight position as a secretary? Investigate the various kinds of institutions where a person might go to acquire an education to become a secretary. You might use the library, your guidance counselor, your business teacher, secretaries in your community, and educational institutions themselves. What are the differences and similarities in the kind of education available at a private business school, a community college, a vocational-technical school, a secondary school, and a college or university? Prepare a paper for written and oral presentation to your class.

3. Write a paper for written and oral presentation to the class in which you describe how a person should go about conveying to his associates that he is willing to learn. Do you know whether or not you are successful? How would you find out? If possible, ask a psychologist or sociologist to help you study this attitude and evaluate yourself. Document your sources.

4. Write dialogues to describe various actions Gwen might take when Mr. Watrous comes to her office. Be prepared to enact the various alternatives for the class.

5. The following characteristics are required by the office worker in conversing with people.

   a. is a good listener
   b. is genuinely interested in people
   c. knows topics of general interest
   d. does not monopolize the conversation
   e. knows when and how to end a conversation

   For each of the following statements, choose the letter corresponding to the characteristic being violated, and record your choices on a separate sheet of paper.

   i)   Appears preoccupied.
   ii)   Inclined to talk about the weather.
   iii) Talks incessantly.
   iv)   Gossips.
   v)   Interrupts frequently.
   vi)   Criticizes the viewpoints of others.

      vii) Enjoys talking about poor health.

     viii) Enjoys talking about own interests.

6. Evaluate yourself, using the following statements. They are designed to give you an opportunity to think about yourself in relation to how you get along with people. For each statement below, choose the letter corresponding to the word that you feel best describes your behavior. Can you truthfully answer *frequently* to each statement?

    a. frequently
    b. sometimes
    c. seldom
    d. never

    i)   I like people.

    ii)   In a group, I seek out and meet those persons whom I do not know.

    iii) I practice and use the names of people I have just met so that I will know them later.

    iv) I am able to draw out a person in conversation.

    v)   I use words like "please" and "thank you."

    vi) I can easily think of topics of general interest for conversation.

    vii) I avoid criticism of others and gossip in conversation.

    viii) I am able to engage business acquaintances in conversation about their jobs, their company, their interests, etc.

    ix) I listen more than I talk in conversation.

    x)   I can gracefully change the subject of conversation when necessary.

    xi) I respond with more than a "yes" or "no" when a question is directed toward me as a way of opening a conversation.

    xii) I readily admit when I do not know something that comes up in a conversation that others expect me to know.

Part IV

Supplementary Case-Incidents

THE SOCIAL-INTERACTION CASE-INCIDENTS WHICH FOLLOW ARE SAMPLES from data collected in the national NOBELS Study from office supervisors covering both effective and ineffective behaviors of office workers.

DAY-
TO-
DAY
INTERACTIONS

THE FOLLOWING INCIDENTS ARE EXAMPLES OF SITUATIONS WHICH OFFICE workers encounter in their day-to-day interactions with fellow workers, supervisors, and customers. Answer the following questions about each incident:

    a. What action should the office worker take in this instance?
    b. What behavioral characteristic is exhibited in this incident?

1. Jane was unhappy with the behavior of Eric, a more experienced fellow employee. Eric would remove a file from the cabinet, look at the file, and then throw it onto a desk. He never replaced the material in the file, even when he was standing next to the cabinet.

2. Shortly before quitting time, Larry was asked to deliver some mail to the Post Office, even though this would make him work late.

3. Albert, an accountant, had gone on an errand to another department. On his way back to the office, an irate customer stopped him and began airing his complaints. Albert was disturbed since it was not his duty to handle customer complaints.

4. Millie, a secretary, received an urgent phone call for her superior from an Air Force project engineer. She told the caller that her superior was in conference and could not be disturbed. She took down a message which she gave to her superior several hours later when his meeting finally broke up. She had made a serious mistake because the project engineer directly controlled

the purse strings on several million dollars of company business.

5. Janet, a typist for two doctors, was being rushed to get out their x-ray reports. Each wanted his report typed first.

6. Sole responsibility for a bonded warehouse, kept under lock and key, has been given to Robert, the parts clerk. A technician wanted to cannibalize a piece because a part of it was urgently needed to meet a job deadline. Robert refused to issue the part because the authorization was incomplete. He held up the shipment for four hours; the shipping deadline was missed, and the technician's supervisor had to leave his work to negotiate with the worker's supervisor for release of the part.

POSITIVE
AND
NEGATIVE
BEHAVIORS

THE FOLLOWING INCIDENTS ILLUSTRATE POSITIVE OR NEGATIVE BEHAViors exhibited by office workers in their dealings with fellow employees, supervisors, customers, or visitors.

Answer the following questions concerning each incident:
   a. What behavioral characteristic is exhibited in this incident?
   b. Does the behavior represent a positive or a negative approach to the situation? Why?
   c. If the behavioral characteristic is negative, suggest an appropriate positive response to the situation.

1. Leona Scott, the telephone switchboard operator for the Gotham City Police Department, was told to radio field units to divert traffic around a fire. She did not specify which units were to respond; and when one of the field units asked for clarification, she said, "Oh, anyone who's around there should go, I guess." As a result, every car assigned to that substation went to divert traffic around that fire. Word of this episode upset the captains a great deal not only because the rest of the district was left unprotected, but also because the police department looked a little foolish having all those cars at one small fire. The girl had obviously gone beyond her decision-making power; she should have asked which unit or units were to be sent.

2. Ellen Sharp, secretary for Dr. A. P. Smith, atomic research scientist for Midwest Power Company, became so upset, when he asked her to place a long-distance call and then disappeared that she had to be transferred to a different office. She had

frequently displayed a quick temper. This time Doctor Smith requested her transfer.

3. Clair Stone, a clerk-typist in the general office of Needham Manufacturing Company, went to the Shipping Department to get some information. The foreman was not in a very good mood and was not very cooperative when she requested the information. Instead of being patient and tactful, Clair walked out and did not go back until the next day. Her supervisor reprimanded her for delaying the work because she did not wait for the information; jobs had been held up because of her impatience.

4. Hillary Carlton, a clerk in the Gotham City Tax Office, left a taxpayer at the counter without telling him where he was going. As a result, the taxpayer felt that he would not receive an answer to his question.

5. Henry Clayton, clerk for the Gotham City Court, saved the city from considerable embarrassment and a possible law suit recently. The court did not have a copy of the complaint against a person being arraigned that morning. Henry called the Police Department, went down there, picked up the reports of the arrest, xeroxed them, typed the complaint, and took the necessary materials over to the court, all in time for the trial. If the complaint had not been in the judge's possession, he could have dismissed the case and, as a result, the city could have been sued for illegal arrest.

6. Susan Aubrey, a bookkeeper for Gotham City Water Works, used to lie about her work saying that the reconciliation statement balanced when actually she had forced it. Since there was no way to check the work without duplicating the procedure, she got away with it until the end of the year.

7. Gladys Farrer, stenographer in the general office of Gotham City Realty Corporation, put aside work that was to be done for her supervisor in order to help someone else who needed a report typed in a rush. Gladys was reprimanded by her supervisor because his work was not ready when he needed it. She was extremely anxious to be helpful in the rush situation, but she did not stop to consider priorities on her time. She allowed herself to be persuaded too easily to help the second person and, as a result, she displeased her supervisor.

8. Letha, secretary to Mr. Whelan, Manager of the Billing Department for Southern Textiles, could never organize her work because she could not decide what was important. When Mr. Whelan was extremely busy and working under a great deal of pressure, Letha interrupted him four times each hour to ask silly questions about her work. Finally she was fired when she brought him a batch of letters to sign which had all corrections x'ed out.

9. One day Judith Weldon, account clerk at Mayfair Department Store, refused to assist one of the other account clerks although she was finished with her own work. She had been told more than once that although certain tasks had been assigned as her primary responsibility, everyone's secondary responsibility was to assist where needed.

10. Beulah Hawkins, an account clerk who was fairly new to her job, was offered some advice by a fellow account clerk concerning a more efficient way to do a task. Instead of accepting the suggestion, or at least listening to it, she cut the fellow employee's advice quite short with a remark that made it clear she was not receptive to receiving aid.

11. When Jeff Biengel returned to work following a religious holiday, another worker made a remark suggesting that some people use religion as a means of avoiding work. This disturbed Jeff. He took the remark personally and complained to the Company's Equal Opportunities Office. A conference was called to discuss the matter. Jeff's supervisor and other company officers were required to attend the meeting and settle the complaint.

12. About a month ago, a stockholder was given the wrong stock certificates. She refused to exchange them for the right ones. Ann, the receptionist, was very courteous to the stockholder although she was being quite difficult.

13. A customer came into the bank to open an account; he wanted to use a bank draft to make a deposit. Helen obtained all the necessary information and let him complete the draft. Then she asked him to excuse her for a few minutes; she went to another phone to call the bank on which the draft was being drawn. She was told that he had no account at that bank. An investigation revealed that he had made similar attempts at several other banks.

14. Allen's new supervisor was not familiar with company policies. He often made mistakes, and Allen tried to correct the errors before the work left the department. The supervisor was appreciative, and never resented Allen's help.

15. Vera Perkins decided that the man who arrived without an appointment was someone her employer would want to see. She took a chance and interrupted her employer long enough to give him a note with the visitor's name. The visitor represented a major city with which her employer was negotiating a contract. To their mutual satisfaction, it was possible to finalize the contract that day.

16. The Personnel Department is close to the Psychiatric Department at Briarwood Hospital. A girl came into the office to apply for a position as a research associate. Mrs. Simpson, the receptionist, suspected that the girl was a patient. She explained to the girl that no vacancy existed but that if the situation changed, she would be contacted. Mrs. Simpson then walked the patient back to her floor.

17. A customer came in for some parts for a tractor. When Marvin, the parts clerk, explained that the parts were out of stock, the customer became quite angry. Marvin listened patiently to his tirade. He then explained that he would get the parts as soon as possible and have them delivered to the customer.

18. Melinda Warren, receptionist at General Hospital, received a phone call from a man who said he had tried to commit suicide. He had taken an overdose of sleeping tablets, but had then changed his mind. Melinda spoke to him reassuringly and calmed him enough to determine his location. She obtained the name of his closest relative and called the relative who brought him to the hospital where he was treated.

19. When Betsy answered the telephone in the Assistant Registrar's office, the student calling asked to speak to the assistant registrar. He expressed concern because there was a blank space on his grade report for one of the subjects he had taken during the previous semester. Although the student was extremely rude to Betsy, she remained calm. She went to the files and discovered that the course instructor had not handed in his grades before the grade reports had been issued. Betsy explained the situation and told the student he would be receiving a corrected grade report in a couple of days.

20. A student whose records had been flagged (a notation of payments owed) in the registrar's office came in complaining that the flag was still there even though he had paid his bills. He was concerned about his image with his employers. Mary Anne, an assistant clerk, took time to explain why the flag had not been removed; the student was satisfied when he left the office.

21. One morning Janice Loftin, switchboard operator for A to Z Manufacturing Company, received an incoming call from the wife of one of the shop workers. The wife said there was an emergency situation at home and she needed her husband immediately. However, she was so upset that Janice could not understand what the wife wanted. Instead of getting upset herself, Janice tried patiently to calm the caller. Eventually, she was able to elicit the necessary information. Janice quickly located the foreman of the shop worker and delivered the message.

22. During a recent period of labor strife, Janice Loftin, switchboard operator for A to Z Manufacturing Company, received an emergency request for a nurse. A plant security guard had been pistol-whipped by one of the factory workers. Janice kept her head, remained calm, and called the nurse. While the nurse was en route, she called an ambulance on order from the nurse and notified doctors. She kept the entire incident confidential.

23. A slightly intoxicated factory worker who had been fired by A to Z Manufacturing Company months ago arrived at Mabel Tabb's (the receptionist) desk one Friday demanding his paycheck for the week. Mabel remained calm and was able to cope with the individual's behavior without increasing the scene he was creating.

24. In keypunch operation, after a card is punched, it must be verified. The verifying procedure is not quite as exacting as keypunching, since the data is already on the card. Wilma Anderson was recently hired as a keypunch operator. Lela Thorpe, a more experienced worker who could have done the verifying procedure exclusively because of her seniority, offered to alternate between the keypunch and verifier with Wilma. Her offer established a harmonious working relationship.

25. A secretary at Martin Transfer Company has had serious health problems during the last several months. On several occasions Marianne Adams, another secretary, has replaced or assisted this middle-aged woman. She was able to console her co-worker and to cope with strains which normally would not be a part of her job.

26. There are occasions when employees in the factory are injured. In one case, an employee who came to report an accident was so upset that no one was able to understand what he was saying. Sharon Manning, a personnel assistant, was able to calm the employee and obtain the necessary information from him. She then called an ambulance.

27. On several occasions it has been necessary for Harriet Evans, a secretary at Mitchell Mining Company, to arrange a conference call so that several executives could talk with a client simultaneously. It is always difficult to gather together all the parties involved. She must often locate persons in the factory or at home. In one case, an executive was on vacation and did not want to come in for the conference call, but Harriet persuaded him to attend.

CORRECTIVE ACTION

THE FOLLOWING INCIDENTS REPRESENT SITUATIONS WHERE SOME FORM of corrective action is needed. Place yourself in the role of supervisor and indicate what action you would take in each incident.

---

1. Dana Edwards, formerly a sales clerk at the University Book Store, was a very stylish dresser and giggled every time a male customer approached. She failed to complete her work assignments, and spent most of her time in the stacks flirting with company personnel. When the supervisor asked if she understood instructions, she would reply, "No problem, I'll do it." When the supervisor checked later, however, she would not have done the work; she usually claimed she had forgotten the instructions.

2. Mr. Anderson likes people; he often stops and chats with the young women employees when he is delivering mail. One day he spent more than a half hour in one department. The department was already behind schedule, and the delay was most annoying to the supervisor.

3. Irene, a payroll clerk, recently telephoned a girl in another department and called her "stupid" because she continued to make the same serious mistake. Irene considered these blunders quite inept and thought the girl should be reprimanded. The girl no longer likes Irene but she is correcting more of her own errors.

4. When she first started on the secretarial job, Laura seemed to have fixed ideas about what she should do and how long she should spend on each task. If someone asked her to do a job, she always wanted to know the deadline, but she would not always complete the work by the scheduled time. Also, she

talked to her fiance on the telephone whenever she felt like doing so.

5. Veronica did not get along with another employee for personal reasons. Instead of going to her supervisor to discuss the problem, she went to the head of the department. Her supervisor felt that she had used very poor judgment and had exhibited a poor attitude toward established lines of communication.

6. Mildred Hackney, a verifier operator, returned a punched card to Margaret Shoop, the keypunch operator, to be corrected. Margaret realized the mistake had resulted from a difference of opinion; she questioned the supervisor about the purported error. Mildred was angry when she found that Margaret had gone to the supervisor rather than directly to her. Margaret began crying when Mildred complained angrily to her; Margaret felt she had made the right decision.

7. A clerk who had been trained to take minutes of a commission meeting broke into tears after the meeting because she was confused and unable to transcribe her notes.

Part V

Critical Requirements for Office Workers

A LIST OF QUALITIES NEEDED BY OFFICE WORKERS IF THEY ARE TO DEAL effectively with people could be inexhaustive. The following list of critical requirements of office workers, developed by Mrs. Lynda Wilms, though not exhaustive, gives the reader a good idea of the magnitude of the concepts with which we are concerned.

Critical Requirements of Office Workers[1]

1. The successful beginning office worker familiarizes himself with company policies, procedures, products, and special terminology.

2. The successful beginning office worker uses proper methods and procedures to perform tasks quickly and accurately.

3. The successful beginning office worker displays an understanding of the content and function of his job in relation to the rest of the company.

4. The successful beginning office worker demonstrates methods of performing tasks to new trainees and visitors.

5. The successful beginning office worker maintains accurate, complete records by checking, verifying, and posting information.

6. The successful beginning office worker operates business machines accurately and efficiently.

7. The successful beginning office worker applies his knowledge of spelling, grammar, and punctuation to the composition, editing, and transcription of communications.

---

[1] Lynda Britt Wilms. "The Critical Requirements for Beginning Office Workers Based Upon an Analysis of Critical Incidents," Unpublished Master's Thesis. The University of Georgia, Athens, Georgia, 1969.

8. The successful beginning office worker proofreads and checks all written communications.

9. The successful beginning office worker maintains and retrieves proper information in the filing system.

10. The successful beginning office worker answers telephone calls promptly and pleasantly using the proper form, giving information to the caller when possible and accurately taking messages when necessary.

11. The successful beginning office worker performs all mathematical computations accurately.

12. The successful beginning office worker works under pressure to meet deadlines.

13. The successful beginning office worker completes all assigned duties without supervision.

14. The successful beginning office worker works overtime when necessary to complete work.

15. The successful beginning office worker gives undivided attention to performing tasks in order to avoid careless errors.

16. The successful beginning office worker displays a willingness to learn proper methods of performing tasks.

17. The successful beginning office worker exhibits initiative in performing tasks not specifically requested or normally a part of his duties and innovates more efficient methods of performing his job.

18. The successful beginning office worker uses tact and good judgment in dealing with problems that arise in performing his job and in working with other individuals.

19. The successful beginning office worker follows instructions given by his supervisor.

20. The successful beginning office worker refrains from gossiping, complaining, arguing, talking back, name-calling, and losing his temper in the business office.

21. The successful beginning office worker assists other workers in correcting errors and during over-load periods.

22. The successful beginning office worker carries his share of the work load.

23. The successful beginning office worker cooperates with co-workers and supervisory personnel.

24. The successful beginning office worker maintains composure and a helpful, courteous attitude in handling customers and individuals outside the company.

25. The successful beginning office worker endeavors to create a good impression of the company to visitors by extending courteous attention to their needs.

26. The successful beginning office worker prepares typewritten reports in the correct format.

27. The successful beginning office worker displays a friendly, understanding personality.

28. The successful beginning office worker communicates effectively with all types of people.

ACKNOWLEDGEMENTS

Many people have contributed to the development of the materials from which this book was derived. First the authors recognize the primary source of data: the *New Office and Business Education Learning System* (NOBELS). The case-incidents in this book were based on the social-interaction critical incidents collected in the NOBELS project.

The authors express appreciation to the teacher-students enrolled in their 1969–1970 graduate Problems in Business Education class at The University of Georgia. These teachers developed preliminary case-incidents and field tested them with their students; many of their ideas contributed to the ultimate format used in this text. The class included: Mrs. Wanda Aldridge, Mrs. Janice S. Chastain, Mrs. Mary Wyl Clark, Mrs. Ruth E. Cross, Mrs. Bonnie M. Goode, Mrs. Jeanette A. Gurley, Mrs. Jane D. Harvey, Mrs. Georgia C. Hobbs, Mrs. Laura K. Irwin, Miss Laura M. Kersey, Mrs. Mary Alice McFarland, Mrs. Addie S. Moreland, Mrs. Beverly Newell, Mrs. Sarah P. Pearson, Mrs. Evelyn Rogers, Mrs. Betty J. Ross, Mrs. Willette Sanders, Mrs. Earleen W. Sizemore, Mrs. Elizabeth F. Slade, and Mrs. Patricia E. Trenton.

Appreciation is expressed to Mrs. Joyce Smoak, Supervisor of Business Education, Duval County Schools, Jacksonville, Fla., who worked with the following business education teachers in Duval in field testing many of the case-incidents: Miss Mildred C. Anderson, Miss Hazel Bloodworth, Miss L. T. Glymp, Mr. W. R. Legette, Mrs. Dorothy Love, Mrs. Emma L. Moran, Mrs. Kathryn H. Mulchow, Mrs. Barbara Patterson, Mr. Harry Pugh, Mr. Charlie Warwich, Mrs. Claire Wharton, and Mr. A. G. Young. Many suggestions made by these teachers were incorporated into the text.

Special appreciation is expressed to Dr. Marjorie Calhoun, Supervisor of Reading Programs, Barrow County Schools, Ga., for researching materials, editing the writing, and making many valuable suggestions as a professional critic.

The authors express their gratitude to Mrs. Mary Alice Simpson, Mr. Bruce Parrish, Miss Dianne Sorrow, and Miss Sharon Robinson, who contributed many hours in typing and retyping the many drafts of the text.

INDEX

DATE DUE